*My shadow is ten yards high;*
*I am as big as the Giant of Cerne Abbas*
*Or the Long Man of Wilmington.*
*I march astride golden shocks of cut corn*
*And between my thighs is all the fruitfulness of the earth.*
*I am the farm worker going home at evening.*

E. M. B.

This edition published in 2024 by Little Toller Books
Ford, Pineapple Lane, Dorset

First published in 1946 by Worcester Press

ISBN 978-1-915068-32-3



Typeset in Sabon by Little Toller Books
Printed in Cornwall by TJ Books

All papers used by Little Toller Books
are natural, recyclable products made from
wood grown in sustainable, well-managed forests

A CIP catalogue record for this book is available
from the British Library



1 3 5 7 9 8 6 4 2

# SET MY HAND UPON THE PLOUGH

## E. M. Barraud

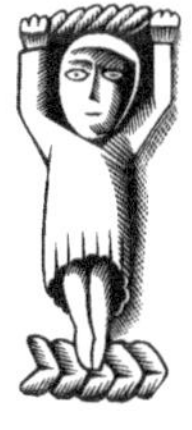

LITTLE TOLLER BOOKS

# CONTENTS

# INTRODUCTION

## Luke Turner

AT FIVE PAST NINE on 12 November 1937, Enid Barraud of 5 Great Russell Street, London WC1, finished her breakfast and a third cup of tea. Over the next seven minutes, she smoked a cigarette as she put on her tie, jacket and a blue hat, and left her flat at twelve past the hour, stepping out into a morning that was bright but not too cold. This diary entry continues to detail a tedious day at a hated clerical job in an office in the City of London where Barraud heard the sound of aeroplanes overhead and wrote of her curiosity that one day soon they might be dropping bombs. She ate a bad chop and roll with butter for lunch. I'd discovered this utterly mundane but oddly compelling needle-like glimpse into the past as I researched a history, now alive largely only in documents, for my book *Men at War*, an exploration of sexuality and masculinity between 1939 and 1945. The diary entry by E. M. Barraud was one of her contributions to Mass Observation, the organisation that in the years during and surrounding the Second World War absorbed a staggering amount of information from the British people about their daily lives as it sought their opinions about what was going on around them.

As I read on, Barraud's submissions stood out from all the others that I'd encountered, especially in her discussion of sexuality and gender. She writes of her dislike of women's clothes shops and hairdressers, stating that she is 'physically female, mentally etc male' and that 'people are people, not specifics of a gender.' She describes herself as an 'invert', a term for lesbian used in Radclyffe Hall's 1928 pioneering queer novel *The Well of*

*Loneliness*. She writes, movingly, that 'bombs do not trouble the nerves of the invert, but rather that terrible silent bombardment from the batteries of God's good people.' Despite this acknowledgement of the cruelty of a homophobic time, Barraud's was an identity that had a defiant love at its core. On 12 July 1937, she writes in her diary of how her lover 'B' rejects the advances of a male companion with whom 'there had usually been some sexual familiarity', a shift in dynamics that she describes as 'a bloodless victory to me'. The day ends in tenderness. B is feeling depressed about her lack of a sense of self, yet Barraud writes, 'she is the most real person I know ... the one person I wholeheartedly respect'.

Fascinated by Barraud's writing, I investigated further and discovered she'd written a book about her time in the Women's Land Army during the war called *Set My Hand Upon the Plough*, published by Littlebury and Company in January 1946, and praised at the time by Vita Sackville-West. I immediately ordered it up to the British Library's Reading Rooms and put aside the usual piles of books, academic papers and wartime pamphlets on queer identity, mid-twentieth-century military history, RAF operations, venereal disease and so on. I was transfixed.

The same lyrical, sturdy voice as in Barraud's Mass Observation contributions hummed across the pages of this short book. Seeing the coming war as the opportunity to escape the city for the rural life she craved, she was one of the first to join the Women's Land Army. On Friday, 1 September 1939, she left London via Liverpool Street Station for a farm in Little Eversden, Cambridgeshire, and never looked back. In prose as skilled as any of the better-known rural writers of the mid-twentieth century, she writes of the joys and hardships of this new life, with vivid descriptions of the farming landscape, people, toil and the time of upheaval through which she was living. At the end of the harvest, for instance, she writes lyrically that 'there lay the sheaves like corpses after some great battle as the sun went down'. Throughout *Set My Hand Upon the Plough*, the war is as ever present as the weather. Her initiation into flora, fauna, landscape and tradition is gloriously unsentimental, strikingly free of a city-dweller's Romantic engagement with a prelapsarian countryside. A bird book tells her that the eggs she's found were laid by a pigeon. As these are seen as pests they are taken home to be broken into a pan next to a rasher of bacon. A dead horse is only briefly mourned, for its corpse will be vital to the hand-to-mouth of the wartime economy, feeding cats and dogs. Barraud shoots sparrows with her air rifle, and along with Bunty (the 'B' referred to in her diary) she grills them to eat on toast. Locals are impressed by both her swearing and her way with a scythe, and she gets her own hair cut by a sheep shearer. She writes, too, so eloquently about her own body, its changing shape, the tan from days spent outside, the callouses from hard work. I wonder if her understanding of and response to her surroundings were so acute in part, because, as the uprooted urban dweller, in her gender, in her sexuality, in her own physical form, Barraud was in every way an outsider.

Barraud had a complex and nuanced relationship with the war itself, which she describes as 'the last suicidal insanity'. Yet it was the war that liberated Barraud from her life of clerical drudgery in the City and sent her to a rural England where, it appears, she made no compromise of her identity. Even though Barraud was unable to write with the frankness she deployed with the anonymous Mass Observation reports, her true sense of self comes out in the firm, forthright tone she deploys throughout, and in how those she encounters rarely or never call her 'miss', but 'mate' or 'buddy'. In the photographic plates that accompanied the first edition of the book, Barraud is as true to the masculine self she wrote about in her Mass Observation diary as she could be. In an image taken at the start of her training as a farmhand, she stands almost awkwardly at attention in work dungarees, face scrunched up under Brylcreemed hair. In a second photograph that must have been taken a few years later, she looks a different person, at ease and smiling with a gun cracked under her arm, voluminous trousers tucked into long socks and boots, shirt and tie under woollen jumper, hair marginally longer, but no less masculine and smart. When Barraud is let go from the farm because her work can be done by male Italian POWs, her rage is undeniable and understandable, a fury about being denied the job she loved and in which she had finally found such great reward due to a gender that she didn't even consider her own.

Thanks to the Mass Observation Archive and Barraud's cousin, David Lumsden, in *Men at War* I was able to connect the writer of entries in the Mass Observation archive to the person who wrote *Set My Hand Upon the Plough*. I had felt wary about this, considering the thorny concept of 'outing' the past, and thinking of sexual and gender identity through a modern prism. I even struggle using female pronouns when writing about Barraud's life, given her statements of non-conforming identity in her Mass Observation diary, but perhaps the greatest respect we can pay to those in the past is to see them as they were, or had to be, back then. After all, her story is a vital one. The queer nature-writing canon is after all still a vanishingly small one; that of the queer rural worker even smaller. I hope that she would have felt content that her work, both written and in the windblown fields of Cambridgeshire, is now re-emerging into the light. Not long before *Men at War* went to the press, I spoke to the academic and writer Pippa Marland, who, it transpired, is also among the small group of E. M. Barraud enthusiasts reading and working today. She told me that she'd uncovered an obscure book of local history about the village of Little Eversden that featured Barraud, saying that she was known locally not as Enid, but John. Was it a final piece of the puzzle? I am not sure. How we understand Barraud now is of necessity a dance between our modern understanding of LGBTQI+ lives, and that very different world of eighty years ago. Whatever the truth of Barraud's true feelings about her identity and the life she had to live in the strictures of her time is as lost to us now as those harvests on which she toiled. Instead, I wonder if we might see the statement of who Barraud was, and how she saw herself, in the dedication to *Set My Hand Upon the Plough*, six lines of verse as direct as her prose, an assertion of oneness with the land. Barraud writes of herself being 'as big as the Giant of Cerne Abbas / or the Long Man of Wilmington'. The powerful line, 'between my thighs is all the fruitfulness of the earth', trembles with a raw sensuality that suggests that in her exodus, E. M. Barraud grew from the soil of East Anglia an identity that transcended gender binaries. Her words glow with a sensibility that reads today as at once radical and modern, ancient and occult.

Luke Turner
London, E4, 2024

*I began my training on Monday, 4 September 1939.*

# ONE OF THE FIRST THOUSAND

FILLING UP MY DIARY the other night, it suddenly hit me with a surprising shock that I'd now been working on the land for more than five years. I started on the first day of the war, and the war has been going on for more than five years, but I think it was seeing the record of other years before me on the page that brought it home to me so sharply.

I've never known five years flash by so quickly. It seems only a few months at most since that hot summer day when I went into the post office in Lombard Street, filled in the form in the *National Service Handbook* and dropped it in the letter box. Then I went back to the office to go on entering figures in the premium register. I forgot all about the form till I received an acknowledgement, accepting me and telling me my registration number was 9,600. We were not interviewed then, or required to give any evidence of our physical fitness, nor at that time were we graded A, B or C according to our social or educational status.

There was nothing else but a number in those early days and by the time a rather sketchy sort of training system had been arranged, I had only a week's holiday left to me, the first week in September. I managed to wangle that my training should take place in my own village. The international situation got more and more tense and the City more and more intolerable, and not only because I was living in one noisy, stuffy furnished room at 63½ Ludgate Hill. I found the weeks only endurable for the thought of the weekends. The BBC reconstructed the outbreak of the 1914 war on 4 August, with that classic tragic phrase of Grey's – wasn't it? – about the lights going out all over Europe. I watched a practice blackout in Fleet Street. The errand boys were sickening us with 'There'll always be an England'. The children were evacuated from London on the Friday and I left Liverpool Street by the 5.15. On Sunday morning I sat in the farm kitchen next door and heard that tired voice proclaiming not peace in our time but that a state of war existed between this country and Germany. 'Oh Ted, that means war!' said his mother. 'Ah!' said Ted laconically, and went out to mix up the cow's grub for the afternoon. That night, a blazing moonlight night, the air-raid wardens cycled round the village blowing their whistles and in the far distance we could hear the wailing of sirens in Cambridge.

We have had hundreds of warnings since then, and many visitations without fanfare. We have sat over the fire and heard the faint uneven beat of alien engines down the chimney before we could hear it outside. We sat in impotent despair as they went over to the Midlands in a steady stream; we heard the agony of Coventry, the bombs unloading just four minutes after each plane passed overhead. Odd bombs from nuisance raiders dropped round us. At seven o'clock every morning during the Battle of Britain the fighters used to sweep southwards to take up day stations nearer the coast. We could set our watches by them. 'There go the boys,' we said as we counted them. And in the evening we watched them fly home again and counted them silently: we did not need the bulletins to tell us that 'three of our fighters failed to return.' One Saturday morning we stood enthralled to watch a dogfight overhead and saw our planes turn the raiders back. One night I leaned from the bedroom window to hear the crackle of machine-gun fire and see a Dornier twist flaming to the ground just over the hill. And now after five years we are still kept awake at night by the drone of planes overhead, only now they are our own, and they are going the other way.

That's the keynote now: things are going the other way, and Dunkirk seems further away now than the day I posted my enrolment form, yet in these five years my whole life has been shaken out of its setting. Back then I was an insurance clerk of fifteen years' standing, earning five pounds a week and with a nice little pension dangled before my nose another twenty-five years ahead. Now I am a farmhand earning a shilling an hour, with no prospects but the Old Age Pension. When I have time to look in the glass nowadays I see a figure that is two stone lighter, hair that the sun has bleached, arms that the same sun has tanned, hands rough and horny. Over my shoulder I see dimly the pale fuller face of the insurance clerk I was, and shall never be again because I know now that, having beaten my typewriter into a ploughshare for the duration, I shall never be able to face going back to town life.

I began my training on Monday, 4 September, 1939. In one week, what can one hope to learn of a craft into which one must be born and bred? I did learn to extract a modicum of milk from patiently reluctant cows. I learned to pull out straw for thatching ricks. That's about all.

While I was training, another farmer in the village took me on for fruit picking. I had a job on the land, was a paid and working member of the Women's Land Army. The nebulous number on a roll meant something real at last.

In the early hours of Monday, 11 September 1939, my employer led me, with what I since know to have been mutual doubts, out to his orchard to start picking purple Monarch plums, and there he left me, with a completely uncontrollable ladder, two cob baskets to pick into, and a bundle of empty half-sieves. I had no idea of the layout of the farm and when he disappeared into the blue to do I knew not what with an unknown possible team of workers, I felt more alone, lost, desolate and incompetent than ever in my life before. Apart from anything else, I have a horror of heights, and of ladder-heights in particular. I have laughed over that day since, but at the time it was unmitigated horror. I nearly killed myself lugging the ladder about. It seemed to have an overwhelming desire to lie down on the ground; when I forced it to assume the more or less perpendicular I could never find the right place or angle in which to set it, and when I did manage to coax it into position, as soon as I set a foot on the bottom round, it lurched sickeningly, with ominous cracking and creaking of branches. I had no idea how many of the twenty-eight pound half-sieve baskets I was expected to fill in what time, but the real sore spot was that in my complete ignorance, and working alone, I did not discover for a week that it was a local custom to knock off for half an hour at ten o'clock for lunch, and when it came to Friday night and I found out, I hadn't the courage to tell the truth and claim my money for those five half-hours.

In the second week, a new terror lay in store for me – my first handling of a farm horse. A man dropped out of the harvest team and I was put on to leading the loaded carts home to the rickyard and the empty ones back to the field. I had never been within three yards of a horse before, and the horses knew it and played every one of their tricks on me. Next I was roped in to pitch sheaves out in the field, and then to help on the stacks.

Those were the days when every fresh job meant a fresh set of unused muscles to break in, till I began to think I should never come to the end of the possible pain and be able to say, 'Now there isn't another inch of me to discover.' Because no sooner were my arm muscles fairly tough than they put me on to horse-raking over the stubble and I got it in my legs so that when at last I dared to climb down from the hard, jolting little seat, I found I could not stand. (That was the day when I first had to stable my own horse and ended up, after a hectic twenty minutes, with his collar round my neck and the harness a glorious tangle round my feet. I have often wondered since what Stone said when he found every buckle undone next morning.)

Summing up those first two or three weeks, I can only say that had anyone had time to realise just how utterly ignorant and inept I was, I should never have survived. As it was, it seemed to be taken for granted I could do this and that and, to save my very face, somehow or other I managed to struggle through. I will admit that when I asked for instruction or advice, I usually got it and I am duly grateful for the patient help my mates gave me when I was learning, but I have always preferred to learn by 'watching points' and in the rush of those harvest days I was allowed to give my preference full rein!

Harvest dragged on, but early in November it really was at an end and I began to wonder how soon I should be 'stood off' and what would happen then, because I had lost my nice, safe office job. The office had been very keen for us all to 'join something' when the *National Service Handbook* came out, promised to keep our jobs for us, and even to make good the difference between office salaries and service pay, but when the war came, things were rather different. Actually they sacked me, in a five-line note, a month after war broke out.

The farm had a German refugee trainee looking after stock and doing all the milking and just when things were beginning to look thin for me he decided he was not really cut out for farm work and left. It was a bitter November morning and I was halfway up my wellingtons in icy water, wrestling with a hedge and ditch that had not been touched for years when the Master came down to tell me the boy had gone, and ask me if I would take on the milking. Luckily I had kept my hand in by milking at weekends on the farm where I learned. Now I had my chance to 'go on the staff' and I started milking that afternoon. Within a week, in addition to milking, I had charge of feeding the calves, poultry and rabbits and the shadow of being stood off even on wet days was lifting rapidly. My proving handy with a hammer and saw banished it altogether. I did not have one day at home during that devastating first war winter.

As early as October my employer had wondered if I could manage the tractor; it would be a help if I could keep her going for an hour or so at a time while he had his meals. He worked with me for half an hour, then strode away to leave me ploughing a ten-acre stubble. Since then I have done my share of tractor work, but I'm afraid I shall never be a real tractor driver; I've never had her in the ditch.

That first farm comprised some two hundred acres, a little of it meadowland, but mostly arable, growing wheat, barley, oats, beans, flax, potatoes, with a few further acres of plum, greengage and apple orchard. None of the land lay more than a mile from the farm buildings. The house was a big, solid, not unattractive place about four hundred years old, with a secret cupboard and beams and big fireplaces and oak panelling. The farm buildings lay on three sides of open yards with another yard behind. They were a miscellaneous collection of older and newer, some thatched like the cow lodge with a deep thatch two feet thick, others roofed with corrugated iron painted a vicious pink. The big barn, which we always knew as the barley barn, was reputed to be older than the house. A lovely great church of a place with huge timbers rearing up into the dim arches of the roof. I loved it best on hot summer days when I stepped into it out of the blinding glare of the sun-scorched yard, my entry disturbing the chaff so that the dust floated in a cloud of golden motes in the rays of the sun piercing through the innumerable chinks in the wooden walls. The barley barn was always fragrant with hay or chaff or the vague smell of meal, and as you opened the door, two or three cats would shoot away in alarm, up on to the hay or running sure-footed along the beams, scattering nervous sparrows who chattered vehemently from higher points of safety.

The stable lay across the other side of the yard, next to the dug-out where we kept our coats and sundry small tools and bits and pieces. The stable always smelt bittersweet of ammonia and echoed with the stomp of the horses' feet even when they were out of it. The stable was Stone's kingdom and the farm boardroom to which we gravitated every morning when the routine stock chores were finished, to receive our orders for the day. Stone would be there first, grooming his charges, and there the Master would find his way from the house after breakfast, there David would wander, and there I would finish up after my jobs in the cow lodge. If the stable was Stone's kingdom, the cow lodge was mine, my first port of call in the morning and my last haunt at night. Apart from the actual milking, I spent quite a lot of time there each day, chucking out the worst of the muck and littering the place with fresh clean straw, mixing up and putting out rations for the next feed and generally tidying up. From a huge crossbeam near the door I hung each year my Armistice Day poppy – there were four when I left, silver-grey with dust and cobwebs. The cow lodge was always a kind place to enter, warm in winter under its deep thatch, cool in summer, and I grew to love it with a special love that I never felt for any other corner of the farm. The rest of the buildings were a heterogenous collection of useful but not outstanding places – the brewhouse, with its deep copper built into one corner, now used as toolshed and workshop, the cart lodge, sundry calf-places, the pigsties, the hay barn with the broken-down root-cutter just inside the door, the chaff place next to the stable, the tin shed out at the back. None of them was invested with any special personality, except the wheat barn. This was the most aristocratic of all the buildings. The walls were kept weather-tight and even as mouse-proof as possible (I spent many a wet day crawling about in the further recesses with a lantern and some bits of tin, the tin-shears and a hammer and nails, finding tiny holes and cracks and nailing pieces of tin over them). The floor of the wheat barn would put many a dance hall to shame. The planks were solid, matured, golden-brown oak with a high sheen on them from the slithering of grain from generations of harvests, and there was always a sweet smell of corn there, whether just after harvest or threshing when great heaps of wheat, barley and oats lay jostling one another or whether, later in the year, only a few dwindled piles graced the different comers. When I was a child, and went to the corn chandlers with my grandfather to buy biscuits for the dog, or canary seed, I used to look longingly at the sacks of various corns, the tops rolled neatly down. Sometimes while he was waiting to be served I would plunge an arm surreptitiously into a sack, loving the cool feel of it and the powdery film on my arm afterwards. I never thought then that one day I should be paid to play with heaps of grain, shifting it about, bagging it up, emptying it out, measuring it, weighing it, and chewing the sweet fat grains as I worked!

The wheat barn always had a job for us on a wet day, and ten to one any wet day would find us there sooner or later, mending or sorting sacks or dressing corn. Although the threshing machine fetches out the grain and separates quite a lot of the weed seeds and other rubbish, there is always still a lot left in, and then there is the job of passing it all through the dressing machine or blower to blow out the carlick and needles and beggars' leece and bellvine and thistledown and dirt and dust.

It was usually my job to turn the handle of the blower. Stone would fill the lovely polished wooden bushel measure stamped with the insignia of three reigns and heave it up to pour the undressed corn into the top of the blower as I started turning. Fans moved inside, sieves shook and soon a cloud of dust would belch from the front and blow out across the yard through the open door, heavier rubbish shot from the spout at the side and the dressed corn poured steadily from the back where the Master shovelled it up and bagged and weighed it and stood it by the door to be collected by the lorry. It always took a few minutes to get the right speed for turning the handle. I would cock an enquiring eye at Stone over the top of the machine. Was I turning fast enough, too fast, or just right? He signalled a slowing down, listened and watched, then nodded approval and my ear made a mental note of the rhythm so that I could maintain it steadily. *One*-two-three-four, *one*-two-three-four, *one*-two-three-four. Often I would find my mind split into two parts, one counting steadily on, the other ranging off on its own, miles away, while I stared out into the yard where the silver rods of rain beat endlessly down. If the numerical bit of my mind got bored it would switch into French for a change, then German and Danish and even Latin – I could count up to four in quite a lot of languages, I found! Suddenly both parts of my mind fused again, and I realised I was getting a bit short of breath. I twisted my wrist a little to free my watch of shirt-cuff. Fifteen minutes. At first I was completely blown at ten minutes and had to signal to Stone to change over. You must on no account stop turning while there is corn in the blower or it will drop straight through uncleaned, and then all is to do again. As I got used to it, I could go on a lot longer. How long *could* I go on? I made up my mind not to ask for relief, to wait till someone offered me a break. *One*-two-three-four, *one*-two-three-four ... I had got my second wind apparently. Stone seldom thought of the human element till it cracked, but with only another fifteen minutes to lunchtime, I felt fairly safe. Stone was never late stopping for lunch.

Sure enough, as the hands of my watch hovered over the hour, he set down the empty bushel and signed to me to stop as the last grains trickled through. 'Master,' he said, 'I've got something serious wrong with me!'

'What, are you hungry again ?' asked the Master with a grin.

'The big 'uns 'ave been chasing the little 'uns this last half hour,' agreed Stone firmly, picking up his jacket, and we made for the cart lodge, there to sit on upturned fruit baskets to eat our sandwiches, drink the welcome hot tea in the thermos, talk scandal and mildly curse the weather. Stone's bristly little grey moustache stuck out aggressively as he gave his considered opinion about the new baby down the road, reminding us that the wedding took place only 'time we done 'ay-cart.' We wondered and speculated about a new feud between neighbours, one of whom was accusing the other of having incited his tractor driver to change plugs to his own advantage. If I had nothing to say, I listened critically, putting in intermittent ejaculations of agreement or astonishment and throwing bits of bread and cheese to the cats which always materialised miraculously at dockey-time.

Then back to the wheat barn where the Master had been patiently darning mouse-holes in some of his best sacks and was ready for our next batch. By dinnertime we had made up weight and David and I were sent to the apple shed to clamber up on to the straw-covered shelves and go through the piled apples, sorting the larger from the smaller and throwing the bad ones into tubs for pigs and rabbits, and making up a load ready for the Master to take to the station in the trailer. In spite of the cramped position, rather like miners at the coalface, this job was jam. We had warm, dry straw all round us, a pile of apples between us, the sweet sticky smell of them thick on the air, and no one to stop us sampling. On the contrary, the Master – putting his head in at the door – had expressly quoted scripture to us to the effect that one must not muzzle the ox that treads the corn! Only Cox's were sacred, and they knew it, lying there in a dull rich heap of Group I splendid isolation. Lass came in to see us, leaving her day-old puppies whimpering in the woodshed next door. Unwisely I called to her, and she leaped to nuzzle me, soaking my shirt from her drenched coat.

The last apple sorted, packed and carried to the pile in the brewhouse ready for loading, it was four o'clock and while David went to find Stone in the barley barn, it was time for me to start my evening stock round. Hens again, and this time I had a basket for the eggs. With all the straw stacked about the yard, the wretched birds preferred to lay anywhere but in the nest boxes and I scrambled and slid and delved and dived after nests all over the place. Yes, the old Sussex had laid in the manger again, and there was a new nest at the back of the chaff and another in the woodstack, and in the old tub behind the carts I found two normal eggs and one, probably the last of a clutch, smaller than a pigeon's. Meeting the Master in the yard, I asked him if I might take it for my tea. 'Don't make a pig of yourself!' It had no yolk.

Then I fetched the wet cows in from the meadow and milked them and set out the milk and washed up and fed the calves and turned the cows out again into the yard and collected my jacket and lit a cigarette and called 'Good night!' to Stone and the others as I heaved into my oilskin. It was still raining steadily. I don't think it had let up all day, and I splashed through puddles as I went down the lane and through the handgate and across the footpath beyond which the cottage raised a friendly eye under its thatch.

People sometimes say they suppose there isn't much to do on a farm when it's wet. I only know I had not been more tired in harvest time, and was glad enough to open up the stove, take off my soaked things, put on slippers and stretch my legs in front of the fire to have my tea, sharing it with the cats and Patch, who was only just beginning to come out of the blue mood engendered by a day in his basket.

I am luckier than most Land Girls. Most of them live in billets or on the farm where they work – I live in my own cottage. I found it in March, 1939, and I share it with a friend.

We used to spend all our holidays and most of our weekends walking in various parts of the country, putting up for the night in cottages, inns or farms wherever we happened to find ourselves, and it became more and more borne in on us that, enjoyable though this wandering was, we wanted to have a place of our own somewhere. It wasn't so easy and the adventures of the search were funny only in patches, and in retrospect.

The cottage is about two-hundred-and-fifty years old, with beams showing in several of the rooms, and a deep thatched roof. It stands four-square at the side of the village street, rather like one of those tea-cosy cottages. Between it and the road is a little stream with primroses on the bank and tall yellow iris along the edge of the water, and good crisp watercress, so that we can slither down the bank and cut a basin-full for tea. There's a young willow tree too, leaning over the bank admiring its own reflection in the water. When we put it there it was a mere slip of a cutting; now it towers above us and leans its branches down round us. The cats love to sit patiently under its drooping branches, waiting for mice to creep carelessly along the bank below. Further along is the stump of an ash tree with honeysuckle swarming over it, and there's another honeysuckle over the small wrought-iron porch. I cut it back with shears every now and then – not that we use the front door much: nobody ever does in the country. We even lost the key for twelve months and it never bothered us!

Most of the garden is behind the cottage. There's about a third of an acre altogether. First a square of lawn with flowerbeds round it, then a sort of bottleneck piece where we grow vegetables, and then the orchard. The apple trees are old and their branches are gnarled and lichened, but the apples are good and every other year we get a bumper crop and send the surplus off to London. Rather pleasing, to see the boxes standing by the gate waiting for the lorry to take them to Covent Garden. When we lived in town, Great Russell Street was not so far from the market and sometimes we used to go along there at dawn to watch the fruit arrive. We little thought then that one day some of the boxes would be labelled from our own address. There are greengage trees too, but somehow we never

*Patch and Missy Ming.*

have many of these to send away; friends know about them and order from year to year, and we eat and bottle so many ourselves.

In the orchard are the sheds, and the rabbits sitting patiently in their hutches, looking out at primroses and violets and Queen Anne's lace. In occasional pangs of conscience, I would love to let them out in it all but if I allowed myself to get sentimental about the rabbits, they would fail of their purpose, which is to augment the meat ration. Only Haakon, the big black and white buck, is allowed the luxury of a name and a personality. I have learned – by force of circumstances and pride – to kill and skin and gut rabbits, but when Haakon's turn comes, someone else will have to do the deed.

If the rabbits are purely utilitarian, Patch and the cats are definitely members of the family, so much so that I dare not let myself enlarge on them or they will steal the whole picture. Patch is a Golden Roan cocker spaniel of the Ware strain. He was not our dog to begin with but took up residence the day the war started, so that he has now spent five of his nine years' life with us, and has been promised that he shall not now be taken away. Ming is tortoiseshell and white – not one of your wishy-washy cats, but with a dark back with a few brushmarks of red, a red dab on her neat flat little head and on one ear-tip, and white underneaths. She is debonair, independent, self-possessed, ingratiating, aloof, condescending, a charming spitfire, and the mother of all the others. Bill started life as Blitz. His colouring is Ming's without the red bits and the black mask above his white nose was so like that of Gentleman Raffles that he became Burglar Bill, and then plain Bill. If you hear anything go crash in the night you just say, 'Ah, Bill!' and pick up the pieces in the morning. He is a clumsy loveable fool of a cat but only I am allowed to say so. Bill is mine. Furpins came next. He is a red tabby, with rich red markings on the palest beige ground. Actually he was given to a friend next door but all the cats make free of both houses and Furpins spends quite a lot of his time crouched patiently hoping for a mouse either in the kitchen or in the orchard. He is a tall, graceful fellow, shy and quiet, the kindest and gentlest of all the cats. Kitting was meant for friends in Devon but somehow we never managed to arrange a through escorted journey, and it didn't seem fair to the railway or to Kitting to send him unaccompanied in wartime. He is a little distant with us, as though he knew he wasn't really meant to live here, but when he does decide to be friendly he can be more flattering than any of them. He is another red tabby but his whole colour scheme is a tone deeper than Furpins'. Finally – to date, anyway – there is Toby, who is all black and who was meant for yet another friend, but his birth coincided with the advent of doodlebugs and his prospective owners felt it hardly right to ask him to start life in a shelter, and by the time the Second Front put a stop to the activities of the V1s, Toby was too big to be transplanted, and too deeply woven into the pattern of our lives. Even had he not always been the most charming and friendly of small beasts, he had a septic paw when he was only three months old, and spent two weeks at the vet, under the shadow of death. Impossible now to notice anything wrong, but I think we shall never forget how he crept out of the fish basket in which he came home, dragging a very sad-looking raw and furless little back leg minus one toe, sniffed tentatively at Patch who came up wagging an enthusiastic stump of a tail, and then looked up at us for confirmation that he really was back home again.

That, as I have said, is all to date, but we sometimes wonder if we shall ever be able to give one of Ming's offspring away – and yet we are always glad when someone asks us to save a kitten!

If it hadn't been for having a cottage of my own, I should never have felt so much part of the rural scene. It makes a difference, to have a real stake in things. Without the cottage, I might even never have joined the Land Army.

*The cottage stands four-square at the side of the village street.*

# FRUITS OF THE EARTH

OUR POTATOES, some ten acres of them, lay late, first because our harvest was a heavy one and then because we had a week of rain and our terrible clay is impossible in wet weather, but at last we set out to get them in. First thing in the morning, Stone and I harnessed the horses, dressing them out in ploughing gear, and disentangled the potato stitcher from its bower of nettles and bellvine behind the cart lodge, lifted it into a cart, and went off down the lane to the potato field. My job was to lead the horses up and down the rows while Stone guided the stitcher or double-breasted plough. For the first hour the horses and I could do nothing right. The tackle needed minor and major adjustments; Short would not keep in his place; Turpin would not pull his weight; I was either shoving or pulling the horses' heads too much one way or the other, and the air rang to Stone's curses and exhortations. I attempted some sort of self-defence, but the horses were wiser in their silence and soon Stone's objurgations became an unchorused monologue. But we did sort ourselves out in the end and then went steadily up one row and down the next, the earth thrown back in a wave on either side of the stitches, the potatoes revealed thickly in the freshly furrowed soil. We paused for lunch in the shelter of the hedgerow and as we munched and gossiped, the field was invaded by a small army of what the children call 'Hairy Men' – lads from the local RAF station. Armed with pails, they began to swarm over the field, grubbing up the spuds and emptying their pails into the carts which had been set down over the face of the field. The first 'incident' occurred within half an hour:

despite warnings, the men had all been discharging their cargoes over the back of the cart and suddenly up shot the shafts in the air and half the load of potatoes had to be picked up again. Stone and I had to jack up a minute and go and put things right and I had an extra five minutes' breather as Stone elaborately explained the mechanics of balance in carts and shook a reproving head at the only half-awed young faces gathered round him.

After another half-hour we had uncovered enough potatoes to take us the rest of the day picking them up. We had to be careful not to overestimate or some might be left lying out for the frost to get at. We tied the horses to the hedge and joined the men.

It was a miniature Tower of Babel working among those fifteen or twenty lads! In a few minutes I picked out the rich cadence of an Irish brogue, the clipped Scots, the sing-song Welsh and the similarly but differently broad Lancashire and Yorkshire. Between these extremes lay the less obvious accents of Devon and Wiltshire and woolly Midlands, the raucous Cockney, and the non-committal 'BBC English' of an ex-schoolmaster. I even found myself acting as interpreter between Stone and the Scots and Welsh; he could not make head or tail of them and kept muttering to me for enlightenment. 'Like a lot o' ruddy furriners, they are,' he complained. 'Jabber-jabber-jabber, I can't make 'ead nor tail of 'un!' I didn't like to undermine his conviction that his English was undefiled or I might have told him that one or two of the men had already confessed they were completely lost in his burry East Anglian.

I worked pace for pace beside a quiet little man older than most of his comrades. He asked me whether I was a native.

'No,' I said, 'I come from London.'

'Oh,' he said as though greeting a second Dr Livingstone, 'not far from my home.'

I suppressed a momentary Cockney astonishment at hearing London described as 'not far from' somewhere else, and asked where he came from.

'Guildford, in Surrey.'

'I know it well,' I said. 'Do you come from Guildford itself or near there?'

'Well, Godalming,' he explained.

I told him I had lived there during part of the last war and asked him what his pre-war job had been.

'Gardening, so this is nothing new to me! What did you do ?'

'Insurance,' I said.

'Going back to it afterwards?' he asked.

'No!'

There was silence for a minute. He straightened his back, reflectively prising the clay off his fingers. 'Nice to have your hands dirty with earth again!' he said.

Then there was the tubby little corporal the others called Jack – a cheery lad who fancied himself handling horses. Stone let him lead our phlegmatic mare home with a load. 'Say,' says Jack to me as he went through the gateway, 'does this 'orse go 'er own pace?'

I broke a switch out of the hedge and handed it to him.

Not the same gang of men came each day – it depended on their duties at the camp – and I suppose about a hundred of them passed through our hands before we got all the potatoes up to the farmyard and dumped them in a great long heap. They had come out well – a nice useful size on the average, but some of them must have weighed two pounds apiece – what Stone called 'regular oven-busters'. Even the chats were picked up; they would come in, boiled, for pigs or rabbits. As the heap grew, we covered it each day with straw as temporary protection against the sharpening frosts, but when the last cart had been emptied the airmen were stood off. The rest of the job was for the old hands. First we piled more straw on the heap till it was a foot or more thick all over. Then we covered it with yelmed straw – straw which had been roughly straightened armful by armful, so that it would throw off the wet. Then we took out a trench all round the pit, cutting the turf and laying it aside carefully. We threw the soil up on to the clamp and smacked it down firmly with the back of our spades, leaving only a twist of straw sticking out at intervals along the top for ventilation.

Stone and I spent a morning carefully fitting the turf neatly over the mound so that when we stood back and surveyed the job, the finished clamp looked like some prehistoric barrow, grave of a mighty chief. 'There, girl,' said Stone nodding his head slowly, 'that old frost won't do them much harm now, no matter how hard he tries!'

For the first three or four months of my land work, my body was so busy adjusting itself to the complete change of life and work that my mind had no time to do other than follow limpingly behind. But as autumn drew into winter, and the digging in the garden was done, and it was dark by tea time, with five or six hours before bed, I began to turn to reading again. Even then it took me two or three months before I had read most of the books I had bought at different times and mentally labelled 'To be read when I get that cottage', and it was not till February that I first made enquiries about the village branch of the county free library. The familiar red torch on the enamel plaque beside the school door had long since caught my eye, and fixed itself in the back of my mind for future reference.

But when I started asking I found that no one was running the library; no one had been running it for nearly two years. Various people had taken it during a period of four or five years, all had given up for one reason or another. My instinct was to rush in and offer to do it myself, but I went warily: I knew that foreigners who tried to run village activities were doomed to failure not only in that particular activity but probably in their whole standing in the village, and I felt I had been doing fairly well so far and did not want to imperil my pleasant foothold. I explored the history of the library for nearly six weeks before I was satisfied that no corns would be trodden on if I wrote to the Shire Hall and offered to take on the job of reopening the branch in our village.

After that things moved swiftly. Shire Hall was delighted and very helpful. It was suddenly borne in on me that I was living in a county that boasts one of the most progressive education committees in the country. Cambridgeshire village colleges are, I believe, still unique. They sent me boxes of books, they sent me attractive posters which I put up on the various noticeboards and in The Plough, and at last came my first Wednesday, and at six o'clock I was sitting in the school, a little nervous but still more proud of my first venture into participation in the social life of the village.

To my astonishment I had nearly fifty visitors that first evening, and more than half of them were almost pitifully glad that the library was to start again, pitifully hopeful that I should be able to carry on, and should not back out after six months.

That was nearly five years ago. Since then I have spent an hour at the school every Wednesday evening with the exception of some four or five weeks in the height of the summer, when I have had to work till dark on

*The Plough is five minutes from my cottage.*

harvest. Even then we have not had to close the library because I found a good friend who would carry on for me until I could take over again. I say 'we' because it is our library even if I sneakingly call it 'my' library when I'm quite alone, locking up the school when my last customer has gone.

To the library, Wednesday by Wednesday, come representatives of almost every household. Usually it is the woman of the house, even if she chooses books for her man too. Sometimes it is a child, sometimes a grandchild. Young Stephen used to come, for instance, a lad of sixteen or seventeen, to choose books for his grandfather, old Bob, who used to do the paper round but is now house-ridden. There are eight in old Bob's family, and all eight of the family 'joined' the library, but none of them read except old Bob, who sits and has nothing else to do, and young Stephen fetches eight books for him every week. What sort of books ? For a long time I was bewildered by Stephen's method of choosing; he seemed to have an unerring idea of the books he wanted, yet they were such a very catholic collection that ... well, it baffled me, and I used to wonder what the old man made of sandwiching Conrad between Berta Ruck and Ethel Mannin, with a dose of Walpole, D. H. Lawrence and Evelyn Everett Green thrown in. At last I discovered Stephen's system: when the old man had read a book, they put a little mark on the fly-leaf. Anything without that mark was all right next time! Poor old Bob, six months ago he had trouble with his eyes, and the doctor took away and smashed the pair of glasses the old chap had bought at a sixpenny stores, and forbade him to open a book till further orders. And young Stephen is in the army now, and I am a customer the less.

Then there is Mrs Peddler, who trots down for one for herself – a nice tale please, and something for her Billy. Billy likes travel books, books about foreign parts, books about country lore, but they must have plenty of pictures. Billy, I gather, is not very particular about the text so long as there are plenty of pictures. Mrs Peddler's idea of a nice tale is what a Boots Library girl once described to me as 'a nice love story without any sex in it.'

Mrs Peddler has many counterparts in the village. I suppose these elderly ladies who like nice tales form the majority of my customers, if you came to analyse them. Old Mrs Cockle is one of them. She adores Florence Barclay and Mr Famol, is pained if I give her a 'man's' book by mistake, and was once outraged when my deputy sprang a real modern novel on her. Mrs Cockle met me the next Wednesday at her gate and handed the offending volume back, with a falsetto denunciation of it as 'not at *all* a nice book, *you* know' and proceeded to enumerate the entire plot! Hypocrite that I am, I smoothed her fluttered feathers; while personally repudiating blame. It was Mrs Cockle who gave me twenty cigarettes at Christmas in appreciation of my efforts as librarian. Mrs Cockle, not the lady of leisure opposite, who has a schoolboy son who could so easily change her books for her, yet always asks me to do it.

Close to Mrs Cockle lives Mr Kay. He was a gardener in Wiltshire as a boy, then went to London, and had retired when the war broke out. The blitzes drove him back to the country. A nice quiet little man, full of amusing anecdotes and lore. He often used to stay chatting to me when he had picked his two books. Then he stopped coming. I spoke to his wife one day. She told me he had suddenly seemed to lose all interest in life, had, in fact, taken to bed. The doctor said there was nothing whatever wrong with him, only that life seemed to be too much for him. I think it was one of the high spots of my librarianship when the old woman called to me from their gate one night and wondered whether I'd bring a couple of books for her old man; he had got up at last, and fancied something to read. It has been fun to nurse him back to an interest in life, and now I usually have a word with him as he potters in the garden. Very odd he is now, with the little bristly beard he has grown during his twelve months' retirement from life, but last week he came out with one of his stories, and one of his pithy comments on the books I had sent him.

Nowadays I seem to do quite half the choosing of the books. So many people send their children down or their evacuees. A small girl of about six trotted in the other night, laid four books on the table. I said, 'Hullo, Maudie, I know what you want before you tell me. You want four nice books for Mummy.' She grinned at me shyly. 'Yes, please, miss: two murders and two love stories!'

Two troubles I have at the library. The first is the colony of young married women and they send one child up to change all their books, but in the meantime they have swopped round down there, between themselves, so that Mrs X's books are returned as from Mrs Y, while Mrs Z has one book of her own and one of Mrs W's. And I have to disentangle it all and mark the register properly, for woe betide me if I try to fine a lady for keeping a book a week late. The village proper pay up smiling but then they always know, and are never late unless illness or death has intervened.

My other worry is the very few youngsters, all girls of fourteen and over, who have left school. Some of them, and a few under-fourteens too, come down ostensibly to change books for parents, but I know very well the parents never read a book and that the children choose for themselves, and such peppery tripe, too. Nor will they, like the older readers, ask or even tolerate suggestions from me. They know what they want, ignore everything else, and what they want is the nearest they can get to the poorer forms of weekly and monthly magazines. I have discussed the matter with the County Librarian who fully shares my view, but we are helpless. The trouble goes back for years and is all bound up with the general question of education.

As far as I can see, the basic cause is the whole rural attitude to book learning – I suppose one might say the whole working-class attitude to it. Traditionally they have no time or use for it; they have always got along very well without it and although nowadays they do begin to realise that better jobs are open to people with better education, it is not through better education that those who have left agricultural work have 'bettered' themselves. It is by chance accident in which education has played little part. Their idea of betterment is to go into the local cement works or into shops or factories in the nearest town. There is a deep-rooted idea that ninety per cent of what you learn at school is a waste of time, once you get beyond reading, writing and the most elementary arithmetic.

There is no doubt, too, that village school teachers are often not up to their job under modern conditions, nor are the school buildings and equipment adequate, particularly where the village school is still locally controlled by the church and a village board of managers.

Then there is the economic factor. Once a boy is past twelve he is a potential wage earner, even an actual one during harvest time and holidays. When he has brought home perhaps 25s a week for six weeks, little wonder the parents strain forward to the day when he will be off their hands financially for good and this colours the child's attitude during those last two years when he might be expected to be gaining most from his schooling. Of course the school-leaving age ought to be raised, and temptation might be lessened by forbidding the employment of children of school age, but this harvest and holiday work is the boys' recognised way of learning farm work and the drift from the land is strong enough already without adding to it.

The pity of it is underlined by the fact that the children do not hate every moment of their time in school. I get on well with children, particularly the boys, with whom I shamelessly go birds'-nesting or shooting or just exploring, and of course I work with them when they are on the farm and with those who have just left school. We get talking about anything and everything and sooner or later we talk about school. Not just baldly like that or they shut up like clams, but I usually manage to get the conversation round the right way sooner or later. I remember I was topping finished Brussels sprouts plants with Brownie, our 'inevitable boy', not long ago. At first the fun of slashing down the plants was enough to keep us going, but gradually it palled and somehow we found ourselves talking about foreign countries. I found the boy dead keen on geography and really knowledgeable and we started a sort of Brains Trust. I am not ashamed to admit he floored me once or twice and when he did slip up, they were not very bad slips. When he found I had actually been abroad a bit, he was alive with questions about this place and that, and the people and customs, and the way they did their work and so on. He was also quite keen on applied geometry but I had to edge off that as he kept on stopping to illustrate his remarks with figures drawn with the tip of his hook in the soil.

Peter's subject is nature study. He knows quite a lot about birds and animals and will pore over a book for hours so long as it has plenty of pictures in it: he boggles at reading matter. I have tried to lure him down to the library, promising to find him a book on birds or animals, but the library is held in the school and he might be seen going home with a book and if he were, his reputation would be ruined for ever! There it is, the traditional attitude.

Young Donald was keen on surveying. Apparently they take them out with instruments, levels, tapes and so on into the actual fields and let them gather data to make their own maps and plans, and Donald admitted he loved it. It was Donald who was put in charge of the final splendid large-scale map that now hangs on the school wall.

John loved stencilling and linocuts, so much so that he could even face with equanimity the wet days when cricket or football were impossible and the time was spent designing new stencils, cutting and operating new linoblocks.

There's something very wrong somewhere. These children are receiving only an elementary education yet they are being taught subjects that were not on the curriculum of my expensive secondary school – subjects of vital interest, so vital that I have had to teach myself laboriously since. And they have really enjoyed learning, if only one subject here and there. But the dominant attitude of scorn is too much for them and they drop it all gladly at the earliest possible moment, most of them never to open a book again.

What are we going to do about it? I say 'we' because it's our problem and a much bigger and more fundamental one than we are apt to realise just now while we are up to our necks in more spectacular issues. It is criminal folly to say that elementary school children do not want more than the barest rudiments of scholarship, that that is good enough for their sort of job and life, that they are happy enough as they are. These children will be taking the torch from our hands in a few more years and if they are not to make the same mess of the world they must be equipped as efficiently as possible. Education in its widest and fullest sense is going to be their best weapon, and at the moment they have not even got hold of it by the right end. Nor is it enough to provide the means for a fuller education; we must see to it that parents and children are imbued with enthusiasm to take advantage of the facilities available. But on the whole the library is great fun as well as a very real pleasure.

I enjoy my hour down at the school every week, enjoy the chances of meeting and knowing people – and I feel I *do* know them, knowing the sort of books they like. All sorts of local gossip flows my way at the library, most of it harmless, much of it interesting and helpful. I order potatoes from one reader, arrange to collect some honey from another, sell a couple of rabbits to a third and put a fifth in touch with someone who will give a home to her latest kitten.

And I have not said a word about the books! Does that matter very much? Have books any *raison d'être* unless it be that they relate to life, help one to live more fully? I yield to no one in my passion for omnivorous reading; it was that passion that sent me seeking out the red torch in this small village, but books to me are an integral part of life, and although I personally derive immense and never-diminishing pleasure from reading and am more grateful than I can say to the really excellent service our county library gives us out in the wilds, it is reading as an adjunct to life that appeals to me, and the red torch has helped me to dig myself into this village, helped the moss to grow more quickly over the angular nakedness of my alien stone.

# TREE FALLING

STONE'S LAST JOB in the early morning routine was cleaning the horses. By then they had eaten their breakfast and in winter only then could Stone see what he was doing. To the stable, therefore, came the Master from breakfast, and I joined them there as soon as I had finished in the cow lodge.

Theoretically the conference was held for us to receive orders for the day from the Master. In actual fact it was Stone who, by tactful or forceful suggestion, according to the Master's mood, decreed what should be done, and that morning he was jocularly forceful in insisting that we should 'go down to the brook and cut off a great load of them there willer and ash poles. That's just what we want to make posties and slats for them yards, and me and the woman may as well be there and get some cut off, then we can all go down tomorrow and the four horses and carts and git them 'ome time David hasn't done ploughing out the headland with his stinking old tractor!' The Master agreed as he does ninety-nine times out of a hundred and went off to find himself a morning's work odd-jobbing. Stone stood in the stable doorway reflectively teasing the matted horsehair from his curry comb as he ran through the list of things we should need to take with us. 'You can 'ave the Master's bill, and I'm brought mine in my bag, and we'll want a rope to draw the poles this side of the brook, and that little bit of broken grey ladder over there agin the brewhouse, and you'd better put some twine in your pocket.'

He turned the horses out to graze in the threadbare meadow while I rounded up the various articles, and ten minutes later we were on our way to the brook. Stone paused for a moment in the shelter of the cow lodge to light his foul little stump of a pipe. The usual joke came out about his flaring lighter, the usual condemnation of wartime flints and wicks (which he called 'cottons') and petrol.

The whole of that part of the farm known as The Brook is my favourite territory. The brook itself is a tortuous, weak-minded little thing, twisting and turning through endless pools and shallows. In summer it taunts us by offering water with no part of it deep enough for a swim, except under the railway bridge. The village boys go down there in summer, but I had not thought it worthwhile until one intolerably hot August evening when I was in desperate need of a cooler. It was muddy and stagnant and the bit under the bridge was rather cavernous with blood-curdling echoes, but it was wet and cool, and it was very pleasant to lie on the grass bank between plunges and listen to the larks and smell the meadowsweet. In winter the brook is a swirling torrent of muddy water tearing down the straight bits and foaming fiercely round the bends, and after snow or heavy rain it overflows its banks and floods the neighbouring fields so that the lower parts of all of them are useless for cultivation. The banks are set all along with ash and willow and hawthorn and blackthorn. The place is a paradise for birds. Great tits hang their pudding-bag nests everywhere and bullfinches whistle and fight, goldfinches flirt and prink and chaffinches chatter. I have seen herons stand gloomily on the mudbanks or in strong flight towards Lingay Fen, and the peewits make a playground of the whole area.

Stone and I were after ash poles primarily, but we also wanted some willows. 'Water weed', Stone calls it contemptuously, but it makes useful if not very lasting posts, so long as you keep your eye on it and snap off at once the inevitable green shoots that appear. Willow seems to strike whatever you do to it. Stone and I even set one post upside down in the ground, but in a few weeks it was sprouting in several places – whereby I lost sixpence in payment of his bet.

I was detailed to trim the brush and small stuff from the poles as Stone felled them. It was about ten years since they were last pollarded, these willow trees, of which the main trunk is some two feet in diameter. The growth of ten years stood thirty or forty feet high, fairly crowded and therefore fairly straight. Yet even the straightest to the eye as they grew proved to be twisted somewhere in its length as it lay on the ground. 'Reckon they all growed in the dark,' said Stone, keeping his eye open for a likely hoe shaft for himself. I said I wanted some ash for walking sticks and he cut me three or four bits of young straight stuff. Lovely wood, ash is. Privately I call it 'elephant wood', the bark is so smooth and silvery-grey. I like the growth of it too, the first pair of shoots springing opposite each other, the next pair springing at right angles to the first and so on; and the buds for next spring lying so tight and lifeless you think they never could open. 'Black as ash-tree buds in March.' But it is tough to cut and before long I laid my jacket with my lunch bag and my hat on top of it. I am better at wood cutting than I was at first, though Stone still shouts advice to me from time to time. 'Give yourself more room, woman! *That's* better now, ain't it? Time the cut gets narrow, you'll be through it,' I laid the brush in a neat pile to be bundled up for faggots, and the stark poles I put in a separate heap, butt ends towards home for easier loading onto the carts on the sloping bank.

By lunchtime we had cleared three stumps. Stone was very talkative this morning and in one of his most charming moods. He can be very charming too – and at other times incredibly surly, bullying and treacherous. Today he was talking about birds, a subject which always fascinates me and on which I love to draw him. He told me again how, many a time, he has caught moorhens with his dog – he on one side of the brook waving a stick above the surface of the water, his dog on the other side, and the unfortunate moorhen staying under water so long that it drowns! He pointed out a colony of last year's 'pudding bags' just in front of us, and a duck's nest on the further bank. He told me about a bird-watching enthusiast who used to tip him handsomely for finding nests for him. 'Ah,' said Stone, brushing cake crumbs from his moustache, 'terrible 'ard up 'e must-a bin to give me half-a-crown for pointing him out a meadow pippit's nest!' Lunch over, we returned to our tree falling. For a moment we stood looking at our spoils. 'Ah, now that'll make a lovely postie,' Stone remarked, prodding a stout willow with his wellington. (I love the sense of rhythm which I believe is responsible for much rural idiom and mispronunciation, whereby a post becomes a 'postie', nest 'nestie', wasp 'waspie' and so on.) 'And that there,' pointing to a stout pole with a strong fork at the top, 'that'll just do for the front of the calf-place where the roof's falling in.' Even I can now see the possibilities in what was once just a felled tree, can see dozens of spits for thatching, hook sticks for fruit-picking, crooks for fruit baskets to hang from, handles for this, that and the other implement, even long slim sticks that I can split up into clothes pegs.

Away from home (the farm is over a mile south of us) and the Master's driving influence, which always brings out the worst in Stone, our little foreman becomes very human. He stands a moment now and again to light his pipe, or just to contemplate the scene while he delivers some succinct commentary on men and manners. He has a poor opinion of both!

I asked him if he was still prepared to take on a bet that the war will be over by Christmas. He was, but only 'our' war as he calls it. He agreed that the Far Eastern developments will prevent a real clear-up before the end of the year, but still maintained that 'our' war was as good as finished. In fact, he dismissed it and asked me to explain how it was people said Japan might be a danger to Russia and to Australia. Geography is not his strong point, but he's dead keen, and in a few minutes I had scratched out a rough map of the Pacific on a smooth bit of ground. He won't forget, either, once he has been clearly shown. It amuses me to think he will probably be laying down the law at The Plough on club night, basing his lecture on my geography lesson!

At dinnertime we took the shortcut home across the fields, and as we went we criticised other people's farming and exclaimed again at the tarring of the little green cottage at the bottom, and wondered what on earth the man at the caravan would add next to his habitation. During the afternoon our pile of poles and brush slowly mounted until by four o'clock Stone reckoned we had enough cut for carting next day. As he stood and calculated in terms of horsepower, I squatted to pull off my wellington and remove what I thought was a bit of stick or dirt hurting my toe. It turned out to be only the seam in my oily-wool stocking. Stone laughed. 'Ah, and don't it 'urt?' he said. 'I remember my wife knitting me a pair of socks and I wore them for the first time on a hot summer day. They nearly drove me crazy so at last I took me boots off and cut the toes right off the humbugging things!'

'What on earth did your wife say?' I asked.

'She just looks at 'em when she comes to wash 'em, and says "Whatever 'ave you done to these 'ere socks? You bin and cut the toes out!" "Yes, I 'ave," I says, and told 'er for why. "You awkward great old devil," she says, and I can tell you we was up and down for quite a while, particularly when she said she'd never knit me another pair, and I said that'd be all right, I'd get Fred's wife to make me some!'

'And did she knit you any more?' I asked, pulling on my boot again.

'That she never did,' said Stone with a grin. 'She'd got halfway through another pair, and she never finished 'em to this day. That's the odd 'un I 'as to cover my flaskie!'

At half past four we gathered up our tools and tackle and ploughed our way back to the farm, Stone stepping out across the field every now and then to see how our oats and wheat were coming up, shaking his head that the Master had sown too sparsely there, nodding approval of the sturdy blades pushing through a little further on. As we turned the corner by the old straw stack, Turpin whinneyed to us, waiting to come in for his tea.

But we were fated not to cart those poles for many days to come. The weather had been unseasonably mild for weeks, and as we worked in shirtsleeves and still sweated, we got heartily sick of Stone's continual repetition of the old saying 'As the days get longer, the cold will get stronger.'

The Master was laid up for a few weeks, and had not yet got back to his normal strength, and during all that time I had been going in extra early and lighting the copper fire and doing the morning milking. Remembering Stone's reiteration, I smiled such twisted smile as a numb jaw would allow me as I hurried to the farm next morning, stooping to gain what shelter I could from the leafless hedges. The waning moon was blazing on the whitened fields, glinting on the ice of little pools and ruts. I had scorned the balaclava helmet when my Mother first sent it to me, guessing what Stone and the others would think of such 'fancy dress', but when the cold really came that first winter of the war, I forgot all about public opinion and just pulled on every woollen garment I possessed – and was astounded to find the whole village come out in balaclavas within a week! Tactful enquiry revealed that they'd had them for ages and been ashamed to be the first to appear in them! But this morning not even my balaclava pulled close to my head and tucked into the collar of my shirt would stop the numbness stealing over my ears, first symptom of the chilblains which will mean skin still peeling off in flakes when hay-time comes again.

I dived gratefully into the slight shelter of the lean-to by the back door, put out my hand for the hurricane lamp and the matches and nearly fell flat on my back as my heels flew from under me. I flashed on my torch. A black streak like some hideous snake lay across the concrete. The pipe from the engine to the cistern must have burst, thawed, leaked, and the streamlet frozen again. I stood a moment, appalled at what I knew would be in store for us before the day was out, then struck a match, lit the lamp and turned to the copper fire. It goes well, and I seldom have any trouble with it from the time I strike the match to the time when boiling water is dancing against the lid, but this morning I was continually reminded of the cold as I went about the job. I had to smash ice on the water butts with a crowbar to get at the water to fill the huge pails, and as I picked up the pails I felt the cold of their wetness strike through my gloves. As I put the pails down, I found the handles had frozen to my gloves.

Having dried myself out in the final stoking of the fire, I nipped across to the dug-out for the milking pails, and went into the yard, the light from my lamp picking out the cows as they rose, stretched themselves, coughed and followed me to the cow lodge. Purity, my little all-white heifer, is a fine animal for the blackout, but this morning she was camouflaged against the snow.

I was tempted to linger in the cow lodge, so snug and cosy it was, out of the wind, straw to my knees, the lamp casting a warm glow everywhere, but the milk had to be strained, measured out into waiting jugs and cans and pails, and then boiling water fetched from the copper, the pails all washed, cloths wrung out and hung up to dry.

Stone turned up about an hour later, driving the horses into the yard before him. I put my head out of the dug-out. 'Morning, Stone!' 'Morning, miss. Sharp this morning!'

'That is,' I said with emphasis and in the local idiom which uses 'that' for 'it' nine times out of ten.

'That is – and the pipes have burst.' Stone said just what I expected he would, and then added, 'Ah, well, we can't do nothing about it till it's light, girl.'

Gradually the east lightened, gradually the moon lost its power and in the twilight I fed the hens, turned the cows out into the yard and cleared up, finally fed the hundred or so rabbits, envying them the warmth of their stuffy overcrowded hutches. As I went about my jobs, so Stone went about his with horses and pigs and heifers. It was not till nearly nine that we had finished and it was light enough to go and inspect the damage. In two hours, the wind had changed a little towards the south so that as we pressed our ears against the straw-covered box casing round the pipe we could hear a hissing and bubbling where the break was. We stared at each other in silence for a few minutes. We knew all the questions in each other's minds, and all the answers. Dare we pump ? We dared not until we knew the pipes were free of ice. If we could pump, would the taps across the yard beat the break in the pipe? Could we get the casing off to see what the break was like? We could not – the screw heads were rusted and many of them broken off. The net result of this part-spoken, part-unspoken conference was that whatever happened we should be without water till midday, for not till then could we even hope for anything like a complete thaw. In the meantime the heifers were already lowing thirstily, the horses stamping impatiently in the stable.

There was nothing for it but to conduct each yardful of cattle to the pond, one after another. David had joined us by now, and we started with the horses. Two knew the way, but the other two were fresh and had to be haltered and led. Then the fourteen heifers and their attendant bull from the front yard. First see that all the other gates are closed, then station David up the lane, myself by the handgate and Stone to drive them from behind, with Lass to help him. It's all right driving cattle if you can keep them all together and all moving steadily.

The trouble begins when one or two turn aside, linger and get lost. The front-yard crowd were models. They even all deigned to drink when we got them to the pond and beyond a nibble at the garden hedge as they went back, their excursion was without incident.

Not so the eighteen younger heifers from the back yard plus Stone's two beloved sows and twelve young pig! So like Stone to decide, high-handedly, that the pigs might as well come with the cattle! They came out of the yard, all among the heifers, at about eighty miles an hour and went flying off in the opposite direction from the pond. David and I hovered watchfully with the heifers while Stone and the dog rounded off the pigs and headed them back, Stone running at astonishing speed and waving his spotted red handkerchief in the faces of the cavorting swine. Very funny, if one had dared or had time to laugh. I have laughed on such occasions, and a moment later the laugh has been against me as the animals I was supposed to be watching have, in their turn, run amok.

We got our mixed herd down to the pond at last, but the pigs wanted to be first, and the heifers refused to share with the pigs and feigned indifference to the sight of water. Knowing they would blare incessantly all day if they did not get a drink, we drove them through the breaking ice into the water, but even then they jibbed as the broken edges of ice stabbed their noses, and scattered in all directions, with the three of us and Lass shouting and running after them. Even when they had at last all had a drink and been shepherded safely past the innumerable gates and openings, we were not done with this wild party. They decided to play 'ring o' roses' in the stackyard and jumped and snorted and blared and danced sideways, rushing round the clover stack and the bean cob and the oats till it seemed they would never tire. By some miracle of centripetal force we at length drove the last heifer and the last squealing pig through the gate into their yard, slammed it shut and fastened it and paused for breath. Stone looked at us sideways, knowing we were both cursing him for letting the pigs upset the whole thing. As usual, no apology was forthcoming. He merely grinned as he wiped his forehead and said 'I ain't a bit a-cold!'

So it went on all day. We were in the middle of hedging and ditching down by Wester Hill, and got to our work only just in time to light a fire to have our lunch. A lovely thing of straw and dry sticks blazing and dancing and warming us blissfully through and through. I leaned over and cut myself a bit of forked stick and stuck it through my cheese sandwiches to toast them carefully. It was smoky, of course, and one side of one sandwich and part of the cheese in it fell into the fire and got ash on it, but as I rescued it in sizzling succulence from the blaze I found it superbly good eating. I sometimes think pensively of my favourite in Paris, the little Maison Voltaire by the Seine, or of Copenhagen's happy restaurants like Tivoli and Lorry's. One does think pensively of food these days. And yet if

I've got to be honest I must admit that smoky toasted cheese sandwich was some of the most delicious food I have ever eaten.

Our half-hour over, goodbye to fire and back to water, six inches of it, ice-cold, at the bottom of the ditch. I slide down the bank, careful not to break the sides. My hands protected in double-palmed hedging gloves, in the left a short hooked stick to hold back the tangle of briars, in my right hand a curved hook, I begin to work slowly up the ditch. I love ditch trimming and it's one of the few jobs where I forget to smoke and am not guilty of sneaking a look at my watch from time to time. Dinnertime always comes unexpectedly when I am ditching. I think part of the fascination is that one can look back along a stretch of cleared ditch and see where one has been. Another part is in outwitting the briars and brambles which seem alive in their uncanny instinct for twining themselves round one's arms and shoulders. Curious how impersonally furious one becomes when something slashes at one's face. One may tear a hand quite seriously and merely suck the wound momentarily, but let a briar catch one across the nose and one is wounded far more than physically!

After water, fire again. My job now is to fork up the trimmings into small heaps, push a bit of dry straw under them, and set a match to them, so that three or four small fires are crackling at a time, whereupon I dart from one heap to another, seeing that each burns out properly, leaving no unburnt sticks to catch in the binder at harvest time.

Water, fire, water, fire – so it goes on all day. And air, biting, stinging my eyes, numbing my chin, catching my breath and turning it to mist before me as I make my way home. Home! But before I can sit down and pull off my wellingtons for an evening's comfort, I must go out into that sharp air again to draw water from the stiff pump, and again to fill my scuttle with coal to replenish my fire. The elements really are elemental to us in our job.

*My own little watercress stream, with Bunty coming home.*

# IN THE MIDST OF LIFE

SATURDAY MORNING. And my birthday. Two facts to bring mild pleasure, but something else teased in the background of my still sleepy mind as I rolled over when the alarm went off. I lay gathering my faculties while Bill purred his way up my body and butted his blunt little nose against my chin. Ah yes! Herr Haenel!

A prolonged spell of snow and frost always brings the birds up to the stackyards after food, and yesterday the place had been alive with them – goldfinches splendid in crimson and gold, chaffinches with pink stomachers and blue heads, thrushes twice their normal size, great jet-black blackbirds with golden beaks, and of course the independent charming robins, and the querulous sparrows and bullying starlings. And even a few pigeons. Our talk turned to the depredations of the pigeons, and the desirability of putting a stop to them, and the shortness of meat, and so to guns. Stone and David discussed the merits of four-tens and twelve bores and I bemoaned the fact that I had no weapon at all. Once again Stone swore he'd look out that old air gun in his tool shed. He'd promised to do this so often that I had come to regard it as mere conversation, but this time David held him to it, and David was going down to his house after work, and David said he would *make* Stone go out and look for it there and then, and if he did find it, he (David) would drop it in to me on the way home.

And he really did. He knocked on the door about seven, and there he stood, plastered in falling snow, a filthy, rusty, battered-looking object under his arm. Stamping the worst of the snow off himself, he stepped into the room, and we held the gun between us and wiped the thickest of the cobwebs off with a pessimistic finger. The metal parts were thick with rich red rust, the butt mildewed and with two cracks in it. The trigger spring was broken or missing, but the actual gun spring was all right, and David found he could hold the trigger forward and get the catch to engage – sometimes. In the course of this discovery he also found the barrel was blocked, presumably rusted up. He pulled back the spring again – this time it *did* engage. He pulled the trigger – and the pellet went whang into the plaster of the ceiling over his head! David drew our attention to his Home Guard 'arms' sense' which had made him hold the barrel upward. *I* commented on Stone's arms' sense which had laid up a loaded firearm! David went home to his supper about eight. By eleven, I had got most of the rust off with emery paper, discovered the maker's name – Haenel Mod. I – the number, and the neat inscription 'Made in Germany'. The gun had belonged to Stone's son as a boy, and was at least thirty years old, and had not been used for about ten. I also discovered that a stout elastic band passed round the trigger guard and the trigger would serve till I could get a suitable spring. Then I went to bed. I don't remember dreaming of tigers, but Herr Haenel was certainly the thought teasing my still sleepy mind at six next morning.

I had no slugs, but I tucked him under my arm when I went to work, just to show Stone what sort of a job I'd made of cleaning him. I was glad it was dark, and that anyway I met no one on my way to work. I wanted to get the professional feel of a gun under my arm. . .

Snow was three or four inches thick even on the level, and once or twice I stumbled in drifts a foot or more deep, and it was still snowing. Still snowing, too, when we had finished our stock jobs at nine o'clock. As usual, we foregathered in the stable to decide on the day's work. Stone and David were to muck out pigs and calves, and litter them and the yards with clean straw. I was to whitewash the cow lodge. This job had been earmarked for me for weeks, against bad weather, and I had already swept down the walls and slats to get rid of the cobwebs, so I darted across to the brewhouse and mixed a bucket of creamy whitewash and pulled on my oldest raincoat, and staggered across to the cow lodge.

The next hour was rather experimental. I got a considerable amount of whitewash in my eyes and ears and hair, and a certain amount on the walls.

First it was too thin, and cascaded everywhere: then it was too thick, and hung in dollops. I got it about right by ten o'clock and then joined the others for lunch in the dug-out. We all had our usual thermos tea, but our flasks remained corked; the Missis sent us over a huge jug of boiling hot cocoa, thick, and gloriously sweet! And I produced Herr Haenel for Stone and David to marvel at his transformation. Then David 'remembered'. He has a head like a sieve, but once in a while he 'remembers'. He 'remembered' now, that he had found some slugs in a drawer when he got home last night, and put them in his pocket.

I let him fire the first shot. For one thing, I wanted to know whether the sights were true. For another, I wanted to be alone when I fired my first shot. There had been enough leg-pulling about it all already. David, when he brought the gun down, reported that Stone had said drily, 'I don't expect it'll work, but the woman'll be as pleased as a peacock if it just goes pop!' David hit his mark, and expressed the view that the sights were all right, but the gun jumped up a bit, and to the right. Stone had a shot, and confirmed this. I made an excuse not to waste any more of the precious slugs, and bided my time. But I took the gun back to the cow lodge with me at half past ten. Stone and David and the Master were about in the yard, so I reluctantly returned to my whitewashing.

The cow lodge has always been my favourite building, partly because it is my particular province, but it is a lovely building, anyhow, with its deep thatch and its great beams and wide plank walls. The bit I had done before lunch was already drying to dazzling whiteness. It was going to look very nice when I had finished. I stood on a box to reach the big crossbeam, where hung my Armistice Day poppies. I took them down carefully before I whitewashed the beam, and rehung them.

Suddenly David broke in on my concentration. 'Give us your gun,' he whispered. 'There's a great pigeon out by the bean cob. Come on!' We slipped through the hay barn, and found Stone standing silently pointing. There sat the pigeon, now on the edge of the barley barn roof. I signed to David to carry on. He raised the gun, took aim, and fired, but the pigeon sailed derisively away, wings a-clatter. Stone broke out into criticism and acid comment. Crestfallen, David handed the gun back to me, and we all went on with our work. A few minutes later I peered out of the cow lodge door. A fat sparrow chirped monotonously from the fence halfway across the yard. I seized the gun, loaded it, aimed and pulled the trigger. I heard a sharp click, and the sparrow was gone. I walked over to the fence. The slug was lodged about two inches to the right of the sparrow's resting place. I grinned to myself, and went back to the whitewash, but Stone had heard, and came to investigate. Modestly, I explained. He smiled kindly, every hair of his moustache entirely incredulous. He stood a moment talking. Another sparrow came to it on the fence. I cocked an eyebrow to Stone, raised the gun and fired again. He walked across then turned and looked at me. 'Not bad – well done, you!' he said, and this time his moustache supported his words.

Herr Haenel did no more that morning, and the cow lodge was finished about five minutes to one. It was going to look marvellous when it had dried out properly. I scraped the whitewash out of my ears and wiped it from my eyes, took off my oldest raincoat, and put on my jacket, picked up my lunch bag, and slung Herr Haenel over my shoulder. As I called 'Goodbye' to the others, Stone had a last word. 'Proper 'ome Guard we are now!' he shouted.

Saturday, and my birthday, and a gun under my arm. And it was still snowing.

I forget what I had for lunch – something quick and easy, and then I left the family huddled sleepily round a huge fire, and stepped out into the garden.

I shot three birds before I was so perished that I had to go indoors. The first victim was a bullfinch. I winged him, so that he dropped like a stone into the snow. I went to pick him up, and there he sat, a hunched fluffy ball of defiance, beak wide open snapping at me angrily. I held him in my hand, and felt very like Mark Twain. I told myself bullfinches were devils among fruit buds; all the same I should not have fired at him had I seen him properly but he was against the light, and my lips were rather tight as I wrung his neck quickly, and slipped him into my pocket.

The next two were sparrows, and I felt no compunction whatsoever.

Their crops were bursting with wheat, and they tear my thatch to pieces at nesting time, and peck the plaster off the walls all the year round. I dropped them into my pocket too – they were both stone dead as they fell – and crawled into the house, frozen to the marrow.

Bill had no scruples about the bullfinch, and ate it ecstatically all over the dining-room floor, growling ferociously and littering the place with feathers. The sparrows I skinned and gutted, and toasted over the roaring fire. Bunty woke up to the sizzling. 'What on earth!' she exclaimed, and then, 'They smell pretty good. I'll have one!' We had one each, with a slice of toast. As she finished hers, Bunty said, 'If I were a cat, I'd live on sparrows!'

'At any rate, they're no more fidgety to eat than shrimps!' I said. All very childish, I suppose, but one must start somewhere. Now I am looking for a small shotgun. A four-ten is my idea, but – like so many other things – they are on the short supply list. In the meantime, Herr Haenel and I must content ourselves with sparrows; one at a time. The snow cleared away as suddenly as it arrived, and at last I was able to finish my breakfast with the curtains drawn back. Not till the end of the month did I see my cottage in daylight except at weekends.

A footpath beside a straggling hedge across the meadow opposite took me, in four minutes, to my farm, and as I went one morning a golden yellowhammer flirted and prinked ahead of me. His little song about 'a little bit of bread and no cheese' struck a big note of sympathy. I found myself dreaming of the cheeses I have so enjoyed, and wishing I had appreciated them even more. The creamy crumbly Lancashire cheese, and the fluid Camembert, the pretty green-streaked Sage Derby and the mottled Gorgonzola – when should I ever savour them again, I wondered? I never was a glutton – I enjoy food too much for that – but I find deprivation tends to make certain things almost an obsession, and dream of the day when once again I shall be able to choose my piece of rump steak, rejecting all but the finest, juiciest piece of point-end, with a nice portion of good yellow fat!

There was a lorry in the farm stackyard as I arrived, and one of our horses, Stone, and two strangers. We had talked of selling Prince for some time, so I was not surprised, though I did wonder for a moment why they had brought a lorry instead of a horse box. I released the cows from their lodge into the yard, then thought I might perhaps as well see what they were doing about Prince, so I stepped through the chaffplace out into the stackyard, and as I did so I saw one of the men holding Prince's halter, and the other seemed to be fondling his muzzle while Stone stood by. Suddenly there was a sharp but not very loud crack, and the great animal swayed, crumpled up and lay still on the ground. Stone called out something about 'Ye're too late, mate,' but as I walked over to them I found myself muttering stupidly 'But ... why, why, why?' because there was nothing wrong with the horse the night before; he was old, of course, but still very useful, a good steady animal. 'Cos 'e's wuth more dead'n alive,' said Stone, but I could see he was shocked too. And there Prince lay, in the raw morning air, and as I turned to get on with my jobs, the men began to tinker with the winch and hawser preparatory to dragging him up into the lorry.

One learns to accept death on a farm, but I admit Prince's haunted me all day. I wondered what thought, if any, had flashed through the great head in that split second when his legs unaccountably crumpled under him as he crashed to the ground. By evening cynicism had intervened: the price of dead farm horses was going up because pet dogs and cats must be kept alive!

My calves were clamouring for their breakfast as I went across the yard. I had eight then, all under three weeks old. Six of them could already drink from the pail without help, but the others were straight from the cow and had to be taught. At first they had no idea at all that the pail contained food and nuzzled me embarrassingly or even sent me flying backwards. Then they learned to suck at my fingers submerged in the milk and after a day or two they wanted only the tip of one finger to encourage them. As they drank, their little tails lashed delightedly from side to side. Sweet little beasts, for all their clumsy obstinacy.

The calves fed, I had to put the cows' tea out and rack up the mangers with hay, and feed the hens before I was ready to start on the real work of the day.

Between the heavier falls of snow we were laboriously draining a nasty water-logged two acres with practically no slope in it at all, so that every spadeful had to be calculated to a nicety to take advantage of the slightest fall. The Master and Stone were digging the drain out; my job was to lay the tiles in position, then cover them with a good layer of hedge trimmings, and finally throw the soil back and tread it firm. Often I was throwing in clay all day, patiently prising out a forkful, heaving it into the ditch, stamping it off the fork with my boot, then levering it off my boot with the fork! For the first hour or two, every ounce of you rebels at the senseless, monotonous drudgery of jobs like that, but you realise (short of employing expensive machinery) there is no other way, and soon you accept it and just go on and on prodding, jerking, shaking, stamping and plodding on. Like so many town-dwellers, I used to think how delightfully varied farm work was. After six solid weeks muck-carting I began to think I might be wrong, and now I know that hardly any farm job is done in a day; it just goes on and on. But after the first shock of realising this you accept it as not merely inevitable but right and proper and even enjoyable. There has not been one job I have not liked, nor one of which I have not, at some time or other, been heartily sick, and yet when the year turns full cycle and the jobs come round again, you go at them with zest. I think the sense of continuity exalts you with a curious, fascinating, fatal exaltation, which probably accounts for the fact that although farmers continually grumble (not without justification either), very, very few ever give up the life for any other.

These thoughts, among others, were running through my mind as I plodded and floundered all day, with just half an hour break for dockey and an hour for dinner. I have kept my townee habit of dinner in the evening because I have no time to cook as well as eat; at midday I just hot up some broth or fry up some cold potatoes and a bit of bacon. In the summer I take dinner out into the fields with me – bread and marge, salad and so on.

At last it was four o'clock and I cleaned my fork for the last time and went up to the yard to milk and feed the calves again and look up and wash the eggs and do all the other stackyard chores. As I went from one job to another I made a mental note that the little black calf was off its feed and might need a dose next day, that the roan heifer was showing signs that her calf was not very far off, that Horace the bullock had broken his crib again. That had to be seen to at once, with a seven-pound hammer and a six-inch nail in the manner of most of our farm carpentry. At half past five I began to clean myself up a bit, by six o'clock I had got the kettle on and the fire blazing and was listening to the news.

This was not quite the end of my day, since it was now light a little longer after tea. First I went up to The Plough to get some cigarettes, then put in half an hour in the garden till it was too dark to see any longer. As I straightened up and took my tools back to the shed, a big grey owl flitted silently through the orchard to his deadly vigil in the barn next door.

*In the stackyard under my bedroom window.*

# SOME MORNING UNAWARE

I WOKE UP BEFORE the alarm this morning, fully awake, and fully conscious of what had awakened me: a thrush was singing magnificently from the slim lime tree just beyond my garden hedge.

It was Saturday morning, and the usual yard jobs had to be done at the farm, but today my mind was pleasantly drugged not only by awareness of the fact that my working day ended at one o'clock, but by the memory of that first waking consciousness. Thrushes seemed to be singing from every tree in the hedgerow beside which I go to work, and great plump blackbirds darted squawking before me as I walked along. A hedge sparrow (we call them 'hedgy-bits' round here) swayed on one of the taller thorn bushes, giving voice to his lovely sweet song – and there was a time, not so long ago, when I found it hard to distinguish the dapper hedge accentor from his wholly inexcusable non-relative the house sparrow.

Yesterday the ground had been white with a second fall of snow. The first had never quite disappeared, and the village kept telling me it was waiting for the next lot, and it did. This morning it was vanishing as I watched, and the sun not yet above the church tower.

The hens knew the difference. Yesterday I had rounded up a miserable half-dozen eggs; today I collected over a score as I scouted from one hiding place to another.

The cows knew. The Red Devil darted out through the yard gate, left open for only a moment while a cart went through, and was down the lane in a flash, nosing at the meadow gate. Very cross she was when I chased her back, and she dug her sawn-off horns viciously into the inoffensive straw stack as I drove her through the gate again, and slipped the cord over the post.

And then, at one o'clock, I made my way home, and stood a minute contemplating my garden before I stooped under the low lintel, kicking off my wellingtons, and turned to the Valor to cook a quick lunch.

In ten minutes I was out again. I meant to dig over the last bit of the vegetable garden. I meant to tidy up the border along the back of the house. I meant to finish slashing back the thorn hedge at the bottom. I meant to sort over the last of the apples, take stock of what seeds I had by me, clean out the rabbit hutches. I did some of these jobs, some of most of them, but finished none. I shamelessly 'pottered', forgetting I was a villager now in my third spring, remembering only my first spring here, when I was a respectable black-coat worker, a despised weekender, thrilled by the novelty of possessing a foothold in the country, exploring my domain as it came to life for the first time. But this year I was not exploring. I knew. I knew the one tiny hazel bush in my hedge, and went straight to it to find – yes, two of the minute red tufts of the female catkins. The lambs' tail male catkins that everyone knows had been out for weeks, but the little red tufts take a bit more finding. I knew where to look, in the hedge bottom, for the spears of the wild arums – yes, as usual one had forced its way right through the centre of a dead lime leaf, bearing it round its head, a triumphant trophy of the victory of the living over the dead. I trod carefully down the little path at one side of the orchard – and found three aconites' little golden globes, their green frills smart round their necks. Just beyond them, the bluebells poked blunt green noses above the soil. A cock-chaffinch shared the excitement, pink-pinking from the old apple tree above my head. I have still to find that treasure remembered from my childhood, when I stayed on a Surrey farm during the latter months of the last war, a chaffinch's nest in the crutch of a lichened apple tree. I have found chaffinches' nests since I came here, and in my own hedges, but not yet in my apple trees.

A bird's nest in your own hedge does seem to put the final seal on ownership. The first one I found was a blackbird's – in the ash stump just near the hazel bush. Luckily the blackbird was a trustful one or she would have deserted: I visited that nest heaven knows how many times a day.

The second nest was a robin's – I ought to say the robins', because the pair have built somewhere in the orchard each year. That first nest was in the broken-off stump of a greengage tree. In 1940 they built in a tangle of aquilegia round the trunk of the largest apple tree. Last year they favoured the southern hedge, just beyond the rabbit hutches. This year they seem to appear most often in the northern hedge, between the third and fourth lime tree. (I have four lime trees, and an elm, in the hedges, which my deeds say I must 'maintain in good and sufficient cattle-proof order.')

I tore myself away from the orchard, and wandered down to what I hope will one day be my herb patch. Thyme and sage and parsley and rosemary and lavender I have there already, and chives. But the chives were rather sickly last year, and I thought I had probably seen the last of them. I scratched gently with my forefinger. No – they were all right, pushing up little clumps of new growth, and the wretched horseradish was still there too, raising lumping heads here there and everywhere. I've forked and burrowed time and again, drawing out the tough thongs, but still it comes. Not that I dislike a bit of horseradish with beef – it is one of the etceteras we summon up to try and pretend our two-inch square of steak is the half-pound of point-end it used to be – but horseradish run amok, as it had been allowed to in this garden, is a rampaging pest and I suspect we shall never quite get rid of it.

Not many vegetables left – a few of the smaller leeks, a rather weatherbeaten half-row of sprouts, and two cabbages from which the heads have been cut and secondary growth has shot out below. Three heads of celery, the tops browned with frost and snow, remind us that only for three more Sundays can we expect the delight of celery, toast and butter for tea. We put up with margarine all the week, to make pigs of ourselves with butter on the toast with our celery on Saturday and Sunday. (How this war has made one appreciate, literally and metaphorically, the bread and butter things!)

We have been very smug, I'm afraid, through all this snow and frost, smug in the consciousness that nearly all the digging had been done before the cold spell set in. And how potent the frost has been on our stiff cold soil! Before we were gardeners, we read dispassionately of the beneficial effects of frost on heavy soils, but not till we saw the sullen lumps broken down to powdery dusty tilth did we realise *just* how potent hard weather can be. It is as though innumerable tiny charges of dynamite had been laid in the soil and exploded. The first two winters, we waited for the snow to go to see what the effect had been. This year we smiled gloatingly, knowing what we should find when the weather broke at last. What was it, seven weeks, two months that the ground had been locked and white? I only know we got sick and tired of the white glare on the bedroom ceiling every morning, sick and tired of the glassy brick path out the back, and of no soft water from the kitchen tap.

But we knew it would break – and the break came in twelve hours.

In twelve hours the snow had disappeared, and the aconites, the hazel catkins, the wild arums, the bluebells and the chives sprang into life. In twelve hours – in less, and in their sleep – the birds remembered their song. But these were not the things that finally convinced me that spring was very, very near. All through the winter I had been able to pick a handful of violets from the shelter of the dead leaves under the hedge. On Christmas Eve I dug up a root of primroses with three or four flowers out, and put it in a bowl and it has flowered ever since, while others have been out along the wattle fence all the time. Now not a violet, not a primrose was to be seen; they have retired into themselves that they might all burst out at once in their bewildering spring profuseness, very soon. And what the disappearance of the primroses and violets said was confirmed by Arthur. He came down about four o'clock, with a screw of paper containing the broad beans he had promised me, and could I let him have the shallot sets I had offered in exchange? And in case even Arthur was not enough, when I came in to tea, Bill clawed up on to my knee for a piece of cake: I ran my hand along his back, sending a small cloud of soft black fur floating into the air. This was Bill's first spring moult.

Another week, in spite of the cold winds, made a tremendous difference to the greenery. Our limes were a blaze of yellow-green now, and the elm was coming out, and even the ash buds were stretching. I had been looking forward to spring more than I ever remember: it must be some automatic reaction to the shadow of war. I found I was not alone in it either: two different people, one a villager, the other an evacuee, separately told me the same thing. And now the miracle was really happening under our eyes. The plums and gages were out, and the apples showing pink-tipped buds.

This valley of ours looks as though the sea had washed up over it when the orchards are in bloom, and then receded, leaving a mass of glistening white foam behind. So lovely to go through the gage orchards, to watch the silly pigs obliviously rootling in the earth beneath, unaware – or are they? – of the beauty overhead, beauty which the chaffinches so obviously appreciate. Lovely, too, to be perched up on a straw stack, to look out over the top of the orchards all white billowy masses of flower.

After work one night, I went for what I call a hedge-hop, just round our own fields, and Missy Ming came all the way with me, though once or twice she got tired and mewed for a lift, and once she got bogged in deep, lush greenery and asked to be found, asked firmly if plaintively, her little triangle of a face raised anxiously, yet sure of rescue. She will go anywhere Patch goes, hence her following me so steadfastly.

My own little bit of orchard was a lot clearer at last, though I was still rooting out old goosebery bushes as their age and barrenness became apparent. I could see all the way up the garden and through the orchard to the wheat field beyond. I even lay in the hammock for an hour on Saturday, enjoying a burst of really warm sun, and till I dozed off I just lay and thought how nice it all was, and tried to see in which tree the tits had nested and noticed that the robins were back and forth to their nest and concluded the happy event had come off, as was subsequently proved to be the case – four gaping little mouths uplifted to my careful enquiring finger. A hedge sparrow was sitting tight on four impossibly blue eggs in the hedge. Everything was vigorously pushing forward, particularly the weeds. I must have removed miles of bindweed, yet still I saw snaky little heads popping up, and as fast as I hoed them off, more came up.

We had been planting potatoes at the farm, back-breaking dizzy work, but at last I did seem to have reached the point where no job could make me ache for long! We had some children helping us. I got on very well with them, particularly the boys. Girls are not so objective somehow. With the boys my conversation was mainly of birds' nests. It was amusing to pit my book knowledge against their practical experience. My own effort at birds' nesting was rather funny. I was out in the orchard at the farm, seeing that none of the calves had fallen into the ditch or impaled themselves on barbed wire, and at the same time keeping my eyes open for anything interesting. Looking into a hole in the bole of an old apple tree, I saw four roundish white eggs. 'Hah,' I said to myself, 'pigeons!' and removed all four because pigeons are an unmitigated nuisance on a farm. On my way home, I ran into one of my small boy friends and gave him one. One I added to my collection, the other two I fried with a rasher of bacon for *my* dinner! Later, looking at my bird book, I found what I already knew but had forgotten: that pigeons lay only two eggs and build a rough twiggy nest. It dawned: owl! I felt a bit guilty, because owls are useful, except the little owl. Let's hope this was a little owl! I was honest enough to own up to the small boy next time we met, but I'm sure he was more than ever convinced I am a little mad!

We finished potato planting neatly on Friday night and devoted Saturday morning to the usual yard jobs. I enjoy this weekly spring clean and the opportunity it gives for being among the animals for a few hours, noting progress or set-backs, making plans for the future.

Mucking out the pigs' places is a stinking job but by keeping a cigarette going I manage to ignore it more or less. Stone and I had a recurrent argument about stinks: he, as pig-man, maintained that pig muck is a clean, healthy stink, whereas calf muck is foul. I, as calf-man, maintained the direct opposite. I think he was as genuine as I was about it. I only know I find pig muck sour and biting. It gets into the back of your nose and throat and stays there for hours afterwards in a quite indescribable way. As both pigs and calves are fed on stuff with a lot of milk in it, there seems to be justification for both our points of view! The bright spots, from my point of view, about mucking out pigs, were the intervals when we paused to admire and discuss the latest litter. I *like* pigs, whatever I feel about their stink, and when they are a couple of days old they scuttle about like white mice, squealing and grunting. William, our lewd and crafty-looking lop-eared boar – father of all our piglets – was as tame as he was huge and fierce in appearance. He had an engaging habit of taking a keen interest in the outside world and all the time we were working in the yard in front of his place he stood with his front hooves hooked up over the rail, watching the world go by. The pigs tidied up, and bedded down in clean straw, we shifted some baby calves from one place to another, letting them have a scamper in the yard en route. Calves are just as skittish as lambs when they are let out, but you seldom see them at large when really young. They spring in the air, all four feet off the ground at once, and twist and turn and wave their tails and dash and shy and are generally delightful. But they are unmanageable, and tremendously strong, and far too heavy to lift bodily, so that the moving which begins as a game is apt to end in sweat and frayed tempers all round and we are all sober enough by the time the calves are safely penned up in their new quarters.

*The professional feel of a gun under my arm.*

# PEPPER AND BEANS

I HAD A WEEK AT HOME, fighting a ding-dong battle with a heavy cold and a devastating cough. My morale suffered at least as much as my body when, after triumphantly surviving a long drawn-out fierce winter, I went down like a ninepin as soon as the weather turned mild and sunny, but there was nothing else to do: I ached all over; and was obviously running a temperature, and spent most of the night coughing my heart out, and eating and drinking my way through an indigestible miscellany of home-brewed and patent remedies, and reading, reading, reading – more books than I have been able to fit into the past six months. In the mornings, I was limp as a rag, miserably bung-eyed, and unable to taste a thing. So I gave in, and stayed at home. 'On the club,' the village call it, because they all belong to the self-help club, paying in sixpence a week, and drawing out during times of illness or accident. I am not eligible for the club but I could, of course, draw on the ordinary health insurance, only this means a doctor's certificate. Our doctor comes once a week, using the best parlour of The Plough as his consulting room. He comes on a Thursday. I finally had to give in and go sick on Saturday, and was not ill enough to send for him, and by the time the next Thursday came round, I was on the mend, and it wasn't worth getting a certificate, with the inevitable waiting period of three days, which would have taken me to Sunday, and then the next day was Monday and I was back at work – and minus a week's money. Ah well. . . Nice to be back at work. In case that sounds smug, perhaps I ought to say, 'Nice to feel fit for work again.' Good to go and let the cows out again, and see the tremendous growth of Christians and, my baby roan calf. Good to go into the stable and talk to the horses, and get my orders for the day. Artificial manure distributing on Gentle's Field, with Turpin in the distributor.

The artificial we were sowing was a compound corn manure – what the men call 'compass', with one of their customary careless malapropisms. I've never been able to find out just what are its constituents, but it is greyish in colour, like coarse salt in texture, and it has an acrid taste and smell as it flies up your nose and down your throat, and it makes your eyes water and your skin smart. And nothing on earth will stop it penetrating every stitch of clothing, and seeping round the edges of the closest-fitting goggles. As you fill the distributor, it fluffs up in dense clouds however careful you are (and you *are* careful when you've had a dose of it). It makes you sneeze and snort, and settles on your chest, and for the time you are on this job you may as well resign yourself to being thoroughly unhappy and uncomfortable, gritty and itchy. It's not much good having a bath every night, and then getting into gritty clothes again in the morning. In fact, the only thing to do is to go all out and get the job over, and then have a thorough spring clean. Altogether a lovely job to come to after a filthy cold, with a cough still about: and I think the fact that I had been 'pepper-potting' beforehand contributed quite fifty per cent to the virulence of the cough in the first place.

In spite of all of which, I still say it was nice to be back at work, to harness up Turpin and back him into the shafts of the cart, to clamber up over the tail-board, gather up the reins, and amble off down the lane, my lunch bag over my shoulder, and Lass trotting behind, her tail wagging.

Nice to be out in the fields again, to notice the woolliness of the hedges just about to burst their buds into green, to see the finches dart along the edge of the field with their dipping flight, to hear the blackbirds squawk as they shoot out. Even a week had made a tremendous difference to everything. The violets were thick, where a week ago they were isolated points of purple and white, and the wild arums no longer spears but glossy shields.

I set the cart down at one end of the field, unyoked Turpin, and backed him into the distributor. Temperamental, our distributor is, and only I really know its whims. We farm workers are convinced that the people who make our implements have never had to use them.

Take this distributor – if only the box were set six inches lower how much easier it would be to empty the bags of compass. As it is, you have to heave and strain to get the bags on to the edge, and then they are level with your shoulders, leaving no margin for raising them as they are emptied. The lever to put the machine into gear and out would never stay put, but has to be tied with string. And the balance is all wrong, so that there was a perpetual tendency for the machine to hang, which means that the girth (or 'wanty' as we call it hereabouts) is tight under the horse's belly and liable to lead to soreness. Before I set off on the first bout, I ran over the thirty-two nipples with the grease gun, and poured a generous dose of oil on one or two other places not scheduled to be oiled, but fruitful of canary whistlings if neglected. Checking up on the instructions inside the lid, I grimaced once again at the appalling English in which they were phrased, culminating in 'The small wheel should not be used only for very large quantities.' Gentle's Field is right up in the village, and one side of it is, in fact, bounded by the ends of the gardens of the council houses. It was along this edge that I started working for one bout, then turned and ran at right angles, coming down to the gardens at the end of each bout. It was washing day, Easter Monday notwithstanding, and Jim's wife was the first one to pop out with her basket and start pegging up the smalls. As I came down, she called to know if I was better, and we exchanged a few words, finishing with my expressing the hope that the compass would not spoil her laundry – the wind which always springs up when one is on this job had come along as usual. Ten minutes later, I was at the end of old Herbert's garden, and Herbert was out there, throwing down corn to his Rhode Islands. He had something to say about the horse – it was Herbert who broke him in when he was young Turpin, nearly twenty years ago – and a few routine grumbles about the scarcity of tobacco. Next door to Herbert, live the Moons, and their younger boy was tinkering with his bike. He climbed on to the fence to watch me fill up.

'Want to earn a penny, Jeff?'

'Ah-ha!'

'Like to pop down to my house and see if there were any letters for me this morning?'

'Ah-ha!'

He slipped down and was off on his bike in a flash. In ten minutes he was back, just as I knocked off for my half-hour lunch break, and went off happily with his penny, while I settled myself to eat my bread and cheese and go through my post. *Very* nice to be sitting out in the open again, really hungry for good plain food.

Mrs Weaver was next, with further enquiries about my health (the whole village seemed to have known all about it!), and then Mrs Dicks, but after this it was getting towards dinnertime, and the washing was all out, and the wives and mothers all tethered to the kitchen ranges, getting the midday meal ready against the time husbands and sons came in, and I was left to get on with my work alone. At a quarter to one, I jacked up, unyoked old Turpin who swished his tail appreciatively, and struck off for home at a good stroke.

More conversations in the afternoon. Dan was out in his garden. Dan is our wireless expert, and he came to the fence to explain the delay in supplying my new accumulator, and said he was bringing it down that night. As we talked his wife came out with a cup of tea for him. Would I like one? Would I not, and my throat parched with the wretched 'pepper'! She brought out another cup, and I was pleased to see that this cup was one of the best ones with a cottage and flowers on it, not a thick upstanding white one like Dan had. We talked of rations, and the shortage of enamelware, and the prices of everything, even when you could get it. 'Funny to have money in your pocket and not be able to spend it!' she concluded as I handed back my cup and got on with my work.

And now I was nearing the end of the field, and admiring once again the neat lawns round Ted's house. His wife keeps them cut, and as I looked she came out of the back door and across the grass and through the gap in the hedge towards me. I pulled up and asked after Ted. This afternoon, Mrs Ted wondered if I could do with one or two little cauliflowers? My own were finished – what the frost left of them – and I accepted gratefully. She popped back through the hedge to cut them for me, and next time I came down I found five nice little cauliflowers lying on my raincoat under the hedge. I waved my thanks and she went on with her lawn-mowing.

And now it was nearly four o'clock, and once again I unyoked Turpin and left him standing a moment while I covered up the distributor in case it rained during the night. The cart was empty now and I backed Turpin in and set off for the farm. Turpin unharnessed and given his tea, I turned to my usual routine jobs for the last hour. Again I found the difference a week had made, and a week of mild sunny weather. A good basketful of eggs and when I took them to the kitchen I found the Missus had got her crates full; she asked me if I'd like to take the ones I wanted for waterglass, and counted them out into a big basket, telling me I really did look as though I had at last shaken off my cold. The cows were hungrily waiting to push their way into the cow lodge and the Red Devil looked round as much as to say 'Hullo, so you have come back?' as I sat down to milk her.

For the first time in a week I felt I had really earned and could really enjoy my tea. I was a bit tired but it was light till nearly nine and the garden in a lovely workable condition.

After the compass, I was put on to horse-hoeing for the first time, cleaning between rows of young blue-green beans over the crest of our only hilly field. First I was made to walk beside Stone as he guided the hoe, directing old Beauty left or right with a shout intelligible only to the mare. He showed me how to steer the thing, going only by the little running wheel in front, leaning first on one handle, then on the other, to bring the implement in the right direction. Under his firm hands the thing looked so easy that I took over without a qualm. In the first dozen yards Beauty elected to wander wildly from the path before her, first to east, then to west, entirely ignoring my frenzied attempts to imitate Stone's wild cries. I suppose I shall never see all those horse noises written down, but to come to the left sounds like 'Woa, come over!' or 'Woa, come 'ither!'; or to the right is more easy: 'Gee over there!' As she swerved, so the hoe followed; cutting into the tender juicy stalks of the beans with a sickening swish. Frantically I tried to correct the error, but the hoe would not come over quickly enough. Desperate, I lifted the whole thing bodily from the ground as Stone brought Beauty to a standstill. 'Don't lift yer 'oe from the ground, girl,' he admonished. 'If you do, you're missing the work, and that'll show agin you till harvest day!' A favourite threat of Stone's for work ill done: 'Ah ... Ah ... there'll be another day, you mark my words.' This and 'He that sows sparingly, reaps sparingly,' are two of his pet slogans.

Patiently, he took over the hoe again for a little while, making me walk alongside, 'watching points'. Then he yielded it up to me once more. This time I did better, and Beauty seemed to be learning that my voice was meant to be obeyed. This time I managed a bout without more than an odd word from Stone. When we came to a narrow row, a 'wheeling', where the drill had overlapped a little, I had to carry the hoe most of the way, making a mental note that that row would have to be done later by hand hoe. A couple more bouts with Stone beside me, and he went away to his own hoe and horse, some thirty yards further along the field, and left me to carry on. It was nerve-racking work at first, with far too many murdering departures from the straight line, and the inevitable sickening swish as we laid the beans low, but I got the hang of it after about half an hour, and found time to look about me. It was a lovely morning, in spite of the biting north-easterly wind sweeping across the brow of the hill. The first swallows had turned up and were swooping and gliding just above the surface of the field, their backs electric-blue as they flashed past me. They arrived a day before they did last year, according to my notebook, whereas the cuckoo was two days late. I hadn't had time to get heartily sick of him yet, in fact there seemed to be very few about yet and I hadn't seen one so far. Peewits were numerous on this part of the farm, and I wondered if I should find a nest this year before the roller got to work. In spite of the preservation order, thousands of nests must be unwittingly destroyed in the routine farm work of harrowing, hoeing and rolling that goes on just when the birds are breeding. Hardly had I thought about the possibility of finding a nest, than I almost trod on one. Beauty had managed to miss it, and the hoe was just coming to it when I saw it and pulled up. Four eggs on a little handful of stick in a dent on top of a ridge. I lifted the hoe to pass over it safely – and I don't care if the work is missed and shows up till harvest! A little later I found a solitary partridge's egg but no sign of even the scantiest attempt at a nest.

By lunchtime I had 'got the how of it' and stretched my legs beside the clover stack, under the wind. Bread and cheese and bread and jam and a thermos of hot tea – very acceptable fare out in the open, with hard work behind and before you and the sun already high in the sky. The war seemed very far away until a flight of Spitfires whistled overhead, flying east. This time last year the war seemed nearer than it has seemed so far, while the guns about Dunkirk thundered and rumbled all day. My brother was out there, and we had had no word of him for three weeks. The guns went on and on and on, night and day and night and day again. Come to think of it, I was on this very hill, pulling docks, when Peter Finney came down to find me. We have no telegraph boy in our village. When a wire arrives, the man at the shop gets hold of the first small boy he can find and sends him out with it. Peter came cycling as far as he could, then set out across the field towards me. I saw his small figure plodding along and wondered what he was after. As he came nearer I saw the bit of orange paper in his hand and went to meet him. 'Telegram, miss,' he said. I took it from him and as I slit the envelope I heard the guns thundering and rumbling away beyond the church tower. 'Arrived safely in England,' read the wire, and my brother's name followed. Peter went back on his way to school, and I stuffed the bit of paper into my pocket and bent to pull some more docks. The guns thundered and rumbled on, but I was free to think of the kid from the office who used to work the telephone switchboard, of the other kid whom at first we nicknamed Lightning because he crawled about so lifelessly; later he became John to everyone, and delighted us with sleight of hand tricks like swallowing razor blades ... John came home from Dunkirk, I heard later: he lost his rifle, his tin hat, his boots and all his kit except his conjuring outfit! Good old Lightning!

The afternoon passed very quickly as Beauty and I travelled up and down, hardly murdering any beans now, understanding each other and co-operating cheerfully. At last it was four o'clock and time for me to jack up, unyoke the old mare, take her home, stable her, and turn to my clamorous dozen calves and stolid cows. Not having enough to do between eight and five-thirty, and with half an acre of garden and orchard to keep in trim, we have just taken a quarter of an acre of stark open field as an extra vegetable plot. After tea, Bunty and I took up a sack of potatoes, and a fork and a line and went to set them on our rood.

*Dockey among the shocks: Lass, young Roland, David, Patch and Stone.*

# ROLAND'S DAY

W E HAD A COUPLE OF WEEKS working away from home, at a farm some three miles off, close to our nearest one-eyed little station, opposite a large RAF depot and on the main road between our two largest towns.

We went over there to cut up some straw into chaff for cattle fodder, the Master having contracted to sell some and finding in the outcome that we should not have much more than enough for our own needs. Cattle market conversation produced a neighbour with more straw than he wanted, and the plan evolved. On Monday we packed up all our tackle, and off set David on the Fordson with the cutter in tow and young Roland perched atop, while Stone and I and all the day's food and Lass followed in the Master's car. The village peered from windows, waving to us, speculating what was afoot; it was something of a triumphal progress.

But it was Roland's day, that Monday. Roland was thirteen, and next year he would be leaving school. His father used to work for the Master, till a growing family drove him from the land into a factory as it has driven so many of the best agricultural workers. But Roland came to work with us every Saturday morning, and all the summer holidays, and whenever any outbreak of infectious childish ailments kept him out of school, as was the case now, his sister having mumps. Roland's pride and delight is to work with a horse. With a horse, no matter what job is on hand, Roland works like a bird from dawn to dusk, but with no horse in the team, Roland is like any other boy, apt to lose interest, or rather to transfer his interest to any other object than the work in hand. His bland and persistent ignoring of the job can be very infuriating when team work is on the menu. No appeals to his better nature will move him, and bullying goes right over his dreaming head. I take my hat off to Roland as being the one man I have met who can resist Stone's bullying, and his technique is simplicity itself – he simply and completely takes no notice whatsoever. And he gets away with it because Stone is absolutely powerless to move him whether by instruction, cajolery, sarcasm or any other means. To reduce Stone to impotent silence is no mean feat.

Monday was one of Roland's off-days. I don't think it was only that there was no horse about chaff cutting, but rather that his world was too full of a number of things. To start with, the Master took his usual job of feeding the straw into the crocodile jaws of the cutter, and Stone went up on to the stack to pass the straw down to him, while I got my unenviable post of changing the bags of chaff as they filled and David kept an eye on the tractor and carried my bags away, tied them and stacked them. Roland was detailed to help David, and to keep the far end of the cutter free of cuttings – the long residue that sifts through over the riddles.

Roland tied one or two bags, then one of the men native to the farm came along with a horse and backed it into a cart. Roland followed every movement of man and beast with critical appraisal. The man and horse and cart out of sight round the comer of the barn, Roland helped David stack three or four bags of chaff. Then a train started shunting beyond the station, and Roland was absorbed in every seemingly pointless manoeuvre. . .

At ten o'clock we stopped for lunch, which was enlivened by the passage of a circus on its way from Cambridge to its next port of call. Great lorries full of tackle, each followed by its family caravan; then the gleamingly brassy roundabout engine, with a lorry behind, from which two fiery steeds leered drunkenly. Someone said it wasn't a bad life that, touring from place to place about the country, not if you didn't mind having no home life. Stone stared contemplatively at the cavalcade. It was some two hours later during a short break to sharpen the knives, that he said to me, 'There y'are, girl. There's a job for you, with one of them there fairs.' I said I wouldn't mind it. 'No more would I,' said Stone; 'I didn't make no answer when that chap wor talking about it at lunchtime, but I've always had an ambition it wouldn't be a bad way of living.' I grinned – and wondered whether Stone would have been a less hypercritical bully if he hadn't always played for safety, and respectability, and a home with wife and children.

Stone said nothing to the point, but after lunch he took Roland up on to the stack with him. Attendance on the chaff bags, filling at the rate of three in two minutes, didn't leave me much time to watch Roland's activities, but when once or twice I did catch a glimpse of him out of the tail of my eye, he seemed to be doing anything but pass the straw along to Stone, and I did find time to wonder what sort of words were being hurled at him – and then I caught Stone's eye, and saw in it a gleam of amusement instead of wrath. I was intrigued, but there was too much din and dust for conversation.

At one o'clock we knocked off for our dinner hour. Too far to go home, so we had all brought our meal with us, and I had brought a tiny methylated spirit stove on which I proceeded to boil up my drinking can of water, and make some tea. Stone watched me, and when I said there was going to be a good bit more than I could drink, I thought he would have fallen on my neck. But before it got to that point, we heard chapter two of the Saga of Roland. As we sat ourselves down for dinner, Stone said cheerfully, 'Well, if it 'adn't er bin for Master Naggs and his men setting up that there elevator, and if it 'adn't er bin for them trainer planes taking off and landing agin, and if it 'adn't er bin for that goods train wot 'ad the signal agin it, and if it 'adn't er bin for that there convoy all flabbergasted' (Stone can never get the rights of 'camouflage') 'I'd er said Roland 'ad done a good morning's work!' David and I shouted with laughter, while Stone smiled grimly under the peak of his cap. Roland went on serenely munching his hunk of bread and bacon as though he had earned every mouthful. Stone said, 'I let him have his fill for the first half hour, and then I just woke him up. It was a shame to do it, but when he *did* wake up he worked like a good'un!' He glanced sideways at Roland, still serenely munching. Then his face relaxed. 'Cor, boy!' he exclaimed, 'air you got the whole family's bacon ration agin in your dockey?' The joke is a bit stale now, but Roland rose to it, with indignant repudiation. The fact remains that Roland must leave precious little for the rest of the family. 'Ah, boy,' says Stone, 'you only got one mother, and she's a good'un!'

And then somehow we got talking about thatching stacks, and Stone told us he had learned the job when he was little bigger than Roland, and from Roland's great-grandfather, John.

'Ah,' said Stone, crossing his legs, and drawing at his stump of a pipe, 'he were the neatest thacker there were; you don't see work like his about here nowadays. Next time you go along that way you take a look at Charlie Black's little barn, where he keeps his vans; there's a bit of John's thacking there as must have stood nigh on fifty years if it's a day. I helped 'un with it. He were a great old chap, wor John.' We sat back, scenting stories.

'I mind once when some of us boys – Billy Eaves, there wor, and old Ruckie, and me and one or two more. We thought we'd play a trick on old John. He lived agin Watson's close, in that there cottage where Kingy Weaver lives now, and one night we got a little old ladder, and I held it, and Billy and Ruckie got up the ladder and tied an old wet sack over John's chimley. Then we tucked ourselves away behind a bit of hedge. Pitch dark, it wor, but old John he came blundering out after a while, coughing and spluttering fit to do isself injury. Making such a noise he wor, that old Ely came out of his house next door to see what the bother wor, and John he swore summat was stuck in his chimley and he reckoned it must be them there starlings' nesties agin. "Kin you see anything Ely?" "No," says Ely – nor he couldn't, cos it wer that inky dark. Then old John, he went and fetched his ladder out of his little old barn, and up he went – and cor, he didn't half carry on when he found that old sack atop of his chimley!' Stone chuckled and re-lit his pipe. 'I mind another time,' he went on, 'when we tied a button on a bit of cotton, and hanged it above his window so that it tap-tapped away there like someone knocking. Out come old John, but o' course he couldn't see no one, so he nipped in again. And then the button went tap-tap, and out he popped. He went on, in an' out like a jack-in-a-box, I dunno 'ow many times. At last he come out, waving a great old paring knife, and shouting, "If I run agin you, if you so much as put your snout round the corner agin; I'll 'ave it off with this yeer knife, you see if I don't!"' Stone paused long enough for us to produce suitable exclamations of admiration and approval of his devil-may-care boyhood, then he went on. 'There was an old chap named Freddie Jones who lived down the lane by the Quarry there, wot 'ad a donkey he used to take fruit to the station, and he'd lend it to a neighbour. Old John used to borrow it to take his gages from the Quarry orchard down to the station. Well, one day we was aworking up the Quarry when we heard a terrible set out. We ran to the hedge, and there came Freddie's donkey, tearing down the lane at about fifty miles an hour if he was moving a yard, with old John bumping and rolling about in the trap behind of him, and the gages shooting about all over the road, and Johnny were shouting, "Stop this damned donkey, can't you? Stop this damned donkey!" and sawing away at the reins he wor, and yelling fit to bring the sky down on 'im, but the old donkey 'ad set his mind on going 'ome, and 'ome 'e went! Ain't got no mouths, you see, donkeys ain't.' He tapped his pipe out on his heel, and slipped it into his waistcoat pocket.

'And I suppose one of you boys had stuck a pin in the donkey?' I suggested, packing up my dinner refuse.

'No,' said Stone, 'No, we 'adn't.' He looked at his watch. 'Not but what we mightn't 've, if we'd a thought on it!'

I don't know whether it was that the activities of Mr Naggs and his men, and the trainer planes, and shunting trains had lost their novelty, or whether tales of his great-grandfather – who had been a grand old chap, and a rare thacker – inspired Roland, or whether the family bacon had given him a new lease of life, but he worked steadily all the afternoon, and at five o'clock when he slid down off the stack with Stone, Stone said, 'Ah, now, you *can* work when you've a mind to, boy. Couldn't have had a better mate this afternoon! Good boy.' Roland was apparently as impervious to praise as he had been to ridicule, but when Stone said, 'If you're dry, boy, there's a drop o' drink in my can,' he had the bottle to his mouth in two seconds and his wide freckled face was blissful as he wiped his mouth on the back of his hand.

And so we spent the last week of July and the first of August chaffing and bagging the straw, a dusty, choking high-speed job of team-work. Stone and Roland stayed in the stack, the Master was on the cutter, David tying and stacking the full bags, while I was putting fresh bags on and taking the full ones off. And on my bit of the job depended the whole smooth running of the team. There are two mouths on the cutter, with a lever switching the stream of chaff from one vent to the other. A bag is held over each mouth by four viciously sharp hooks. When the cutter is working all out, the bags fill in about forty seconds, so that I had forty seconds in which to unhook the full bag, drag it out of the way, pick up and hook on a new bag, and swing over the lever. And the bags are usually too long to hang clear of the ground so that they have to be shaken, lifted and bumped, and kept on the move to ensure that they get properly filled. Add to this that the bags were not all the same shape or size, and that some were potato bags, altogether too small to go on to the machine and you will realise I was kept moving, but you will not realise just how I had to hop about, keeping an eye on each filling bag, ready at a moment's notice to swing the lever over for a few seconds while I shook the filling bag, ready to thrust my arm up and release a temporary jam, ready to snatch a too-small bag out of the way and find another, and another – all too small – and try and get one proper-sized one on the hooks before the first bag was full. Sometimes I failed, as once when I struck about a dozen small bags in succession (they are all screwed up so that you can't tell till you pick them up), and then I had to catch hold of the Master's foot and signal a halt: the noise of the tractor and cutter made speech impossible. Fortunately the cutter knives need 'sharping' about once an hour, and this gives a necessary breather, but I found it worthwhile using some of my rest time to go through the next batch of bags and throw out the smalls. Do you know the difference between a bag and a sack? It's not only size, but texture and material. A sack is an altogether superior thing, its *raison d'être* being to hold grain – oats, barley, wheat. It is close woven, of good strong stuff. A bag is, roughly, anything else that looks like a sack! Looser woven, poorer material altogether. You may occasionally get sack material and weave, but smaller in size than the standard sack, and these we call bags too. A sack is a sack till it falls to pieces, and then the pieces are treasured to patch other sacks, but a bag is only a bag, even though wartime shortage has made us careful and respectful so that they are getting a bit above themselves.

The last bag of chaffed hay was unhooked at last, and the debris cleared up, the cutter dragged away and covered over, and towed home. And then we went to the oats, and Stone sharped his scythe, and tucked his rub bag on his belt, and stooped to cut the first swathe of the harvest. On to horkey, the immemorial harvest home! My job was to go behind him, gathering up the fallen stalks into bundles about the size of a sheaf, binding them up with a wisp of oats, throwing them well to the side, out of the way of the binder, already being tuned up on the end of the roadway. This was a new job for me, although this was my third harvest, and it took me a little while to 'get the how' of it. As Stone said – and I grinned sheepish self-satisfaction – 'It don't usually take me long to show *you* anything,' and he is very good at explaining the why, as well as just showing the how. He shows me how his scythe carries one cut to the back, the next just forward, one back, next forward, so that my job was to pull each handful towards me in the order in which he cut them. This grasped, my bundles became coherent, instead of being a meaningless jangle of stalks and ears as they were at first. And then the tying: a wisp of about a dozen stalks, raise the bundles against my shins with the left hand, thrust the ears' end of the wisp under and towards me with the right, seize the stalk ends with my left, bring my hands sharply together with a thrust and a twist to make the bundle tight, twist stalk end round ears once or twice, and tuck under the band with a thrust of the knuckles. And now I was all right, and away we went round the rim of the nine-acre field, with only a pause now and then for Stone to sharpen his blade and exchange comments with me. Patch was following close, nosing along the edge of the cut corn, and once he put up a covey of young partridges and darted after them into the corn – they could only flutter – but he was too slow, and came out again further up the field, panting and tongue hanging out, looking a bit silly and self-conscious.

In two days, we had gathered and tied round the two oat fields, and before we had finished the second, the binder was travelling round the first, sails whirling, sheaves falling off every few seconds, and when it left the field, there lay the sheaves like corpses after some great battle as the sun went down.

Shocking came next, and for this we turned out a full team, or rather three teams of three apiece. I was with Stone and Roland and Stone led the way, lifting two sheaves, one under each arm, marching ahead, turning, setting them down firmly on the ground, butts apart, ears together. Succinctly, he issued his instructions to his team: 'Bolch the arse on the ground and smack their 'eads togither!' And so we went round and round the field, each team taking six rows of fallen sheaves, so that we took up eighteen rows at a round. Stone, as expert, set up our first pair, then I came along with mine and clapped them down at one end of his, slightly leaning towards them, and the boy clapped his at the other end. Six sheaves to a shock is minimum; we usually put eight or ten for added strength. A sudden thunder shower sent us scuttling to cover, and we all crawled in under the tarpaulin over the binder. Fortunately the shower did not last long or we should have been soaked as we lay, for the rain and hail poured on to the metal sheet at the base of the binder so that we found ourselves sitting in two inches of water! Had we not almost finished the field we should have jacked up when the rain came, but we had only the centre bit left, so we went on. Even in the short time required to finish setting up the field we were soaked to the skin as we carried the drenched sheaves between our arms and our bodies.

At last the job was done and we stood and surveyed the field for a minute before making for the farm and home and tea. 'Nice bit of oats, Master,' said Stone approvingly. '*Nice* bit of oats!'

'Not so bad,' says Master.

There they stand in sturdy rows, no longer corpses, but soldiers ready for battle, the oats for which I helped to plough, and cultivate, and drill and roll and hoe, and pull docks. And if the enemy came out of the sky in the darkness, with flaming destruction, these soldiers would not be left alone to be surprised: tonight we took our first spell of harvest fire-watching patrol. They might become *your* winter porridge, but now they were *our* oats, and we who tended them and watched them from seed-time through to harvest volunteered without waiting to be asked to watch them through the nights. When you stir your porridge, think of those sheaves standing firm as rocks, yet with gay scarlet poppies and blue scabious and wreaths of columbine tucked in their waistbands. And if you have a minute to spare, think, too, of us. 'With what wisdom shall he be furnished that holdeth the plough. . .?' I was again reminded of this, which formed part of the lesson at my first harvest festival, as I worked carting wheat from Low Close. Our farm team consisted of the Master, Stone, David, young Roland and myself – two men, two boys and a woman. But for harvest we got help from the nearest military camp. They came two or three or a dozen, for an hour or a morning or an afternoon according to the exigencies of duties and fatigues.

Sometimes the same gang came two or three times running, then we missed them just as we were used to them, and strangers came. They were from all parts of the country, echoing accents of Lancashire, Yorkshire, Scotland, Ireland, Wales, Cockney London, the Shires and all the soft West Country. And they came from all trades – miners with the tiny blue pit scars on their faces, mill hands, iron founders, carpenters, window cleaners, and some of them agricultural workers. Put a man on a stack, or down in the field with an empty cart and you soon light joyfully on those who have handled a pitchfork before.

Take Jock. We simply had to have our own regular team up at the stackyard, and the Master turned to the latest batch of soldiers and looked round. 'Any of you know anything about loading a cart?' he asked with a pessimistic grin.

'I kin put up a wee bit,' says Jock quietly. We packed him off, hoping not much. Twenty minutes later old Turpin came nodding up the road, drawing behind him a beautifully balanced towering load of corn. We stopped working to admire it. So Jock could 'put up a wee bit,' could he? Every sheaf was nicely placed, 'like herrings in a box' as Stone put it, and Stone is grudging with his praise.

Then there was the lanky silent lad we called Norfolk after his native county. He said he'd worked a bit on a farm when he was a lad. His loads, too, were lovely things – lovely in themselves, let alone by comparison with the poor hanging hotch-potches we had been having from brawny, well-meaning but inept townsmen all the morning. And Norman, from Durham County. He had quite a different style of loading, but his loads were beautifully made, on great wide bases, like boats riding the bosom of the sea.

It so happened that for those two days I was driving – taking empty carts down to the field a mile from home, bringing back the full loads, and often I had to wait a few minutes in the field while they topped up. I enjoyed watching the different styles from different parts of the country, enjoyed talking to the men about the work. And all the time I was being struck by their attitudes to us farm workers, and annoyed to find myself on the defensive so often, till by the end of the day I was half dispirited. They obviously thought us fools to work so hard, such long grim hours in all weathers, for so little money. Were they right? Or were we?

As it happened, only that morning the Master, commenting on some job on hand, had told me he had just had his bank statement – the net result of which was that we were £100 down on the position twelve months earlier! And this in time of war, when agriculture is regarded as the fourth line of defence and protected and helped to the utmost.

What is to be done about agriculture? What is wrong? Can it be put right, or is farming in England to be regarded as a wholly uneconomic proposition and allowed to become extinct, save perhaps as a picturesque craft practised only by a few rich men more or less as a hobby, in small 'preserves'? I suppose I am rushing in where angels fear to tread even to raise such questions once again – I who have had only five short years and know only the crudest rudiments of the thing, and yet maybe a newcomer, used to other commercial undertakings, can see a little that the man who has been in it all his life overlooks. I see the long hours, the unresting hectic effort of certain seasons, the slack periods, the wretched pay. I see, too, the devastating effects of the wrong weather, the terrific overheads, the returns coming in in bits and pieces. There is so much that is unpredictable, so much that the most careful planning cannot take into account, that the whole business becomes seventy-five per cent gamble, and only twenty-five per cent organisation. The miracle is that so many men go on farming, as their fathers did before them, that so many labourers remain on the land, and it isn't only the slow-witted, the duds. The more I see of the average countryman, the more I am sure that his slowness is the slowness of certainty: all his life he has pitted his wits and his strength against nature and his wisdom is fundamental, his adaptability the adaptability of one whose every nerve is alert for every move of the enemy, to forestall those of which he receives the slightest hint, to grapple with those which spring upon him unawares. It is in his blood, has been in his blood for generations, and he would not be happy, would not fit in anywhere else, at any other job. That is why he stays, and fights every inch of the way, every day of his life. It is the fight that counts, the fight that is its own reward, that carries in itself its own wisdom.

And because it is so fundamental, so ingrained and primitive an instinct, when the countryman is faced with the townsman's 'Why?' he hesitates, cannot explain himself, and is dumb as though there *were* no answer. To him, to ask him why he stays on the land, endures and fights, is as though you asked him, 'Why are you alive?' He does not know the answer, not in words. Ecclesiasticus knew, though. Later on in that same thirty-eighth chapter he gives it: 'All these trust to their hands, and every one is wise in his own art. Without these the city is not built ... Upon the judge's seat they shall not sit ... and they shall not be found where parables are spoken but they shall strengthen the state of the world and their prayer shall be in the work of their craft.' And if I felt tempted to say to myself, 'Ah, but Ecclesiasticus was a wise man himself, a thinker, not a practical man; maybe he was unreasonably abstract,' suddenly I remembered Jock with his 'wee bit' – he had been on a farm till he got a better job; and Norfolk who had worked on the land till a wife and three children forced him into better paid work. I remembered Jock's shy pride as we praised his loads, his quiet 'Ay, it's a braw life, this.' I remembered Norfolk's sweat-grimed face at the end of the day as he pulled on his rough khaki jacket, and his wistful remark, 'Mebbe I'll get back to the farm afore I die!' There was the answer – there, and in our four-square stacks.

If you've got stock about a farm, they are apt to pay no heed to other jobs on hand, and to demand urgent attention at a moment's notice.

We had about a dozen young heifers nearing maturity, and suddenly it became apparent that they were ready for mating. As I turned the corner by the dug-out I met Stone coming from feeding the pigs. He clattered his empty pails to the ground by the drum shed and greeted me with 'Master wants you to get your jobs done soon as maybe, then we're going to Gent Baker's to fetch his young bull to them 'eifers. We'll take the Red Devil and the little white 'eifer to fetch him back.' Further exhortations to speed followed me as I made my way to the cow lodge.

By a quarter to nine Stone and I and Patch were setting off down the lane. It was a lovely morning, with great billowy clouds scudding across the sky from the south-west. Stone forecast rain before the end of the day, but then he had been forecasting thunder for the past week: he said there was always a storm about the time of Barringford Feast which was that weekend.

We had our first anxious moment at the top of the lane, shepherding the little white heifer who made a dive for the gap in the hedge where the Master's daughter had plunged the tractor through, but we soon put things right and the little heifer followed the Red Devil placidly enough along the road. Concentration was necessary for the next half mile. First the crossroads by 'The Hoops': only two of us to guard four possible deviations, but we knew this danger of old and took our small herd past it at the double. More subtle was the length of road past the shop, with two gates, both open (naturally!) and a cart entrance, but once again we were lucky, and then our troubles were over, with only a straight run past three cottages and up to the gates of Baker's yard.

The bull was out in the close behind the farm buildings and we had to find the stockman to fetch him in for us. He came demurely enough and took no notice whatever of the Red Devil and the little white heifer who were nosing about curiously in the strange yard.

If the journey outward had been uneventful, the journey back was packed with what the news bulletins call 'incidents'. Our cows knew the way home and were already bored with the rather pointless expedition. They forged ahead and Patch and I had to keep darting forward to slow them up. The bull, on the other hand, had left his home and an attentive escort of lady friends, and as we came away they ran along the other side of the hedge exclaiming and upbraiding. Nor was he unmoved by their appeals, and made repeated efforts to crash through the somewhat scanty hedge – all of which only added to the growing distance between our homing cows and his reluctant self. Then came the shop and the gateway at the side. I had run ahead, on Stone's urgent order, and shut the gate and returned to my responsibility of restraining the cows. The bull made straight for the gateway. Knowing it firmly shut, Stone and I smiled cheerfully. The bull took that gate 'like a ruddy grey'ound' as Stone put it later, and Stone dashed after him, shouting highly coloured warnings to whomever might be about. As I went to help him I saw the frenzied legs of Mrs Clement dashing for the safety of the kitchen door.

Our charge came out quietly enough, and made straight across the road and through a decrepit fence into the old recreation ground. By this time the cows were tossing up which road to take by 'The Hoops' but Stone and I were beyond bothering about them. It took us ten minutes to get the bull back on to the road – at least, we got him out three times in ten minutes and each time he slipped back again through different places in the derelict fence. Apparently by that time he was as tired of the manoeuvre as we were. He changed his tactics and made for the other side of the road some fifty yards beyond the shop and darted into a gateway. The gate was shut and much too high for jumping, but from standing he leaped over some four-foot-high spiked iron railings into a tiny enclosure just big enough to take him, not big enough for him to turn in. This looked like checkmate and Stone and I took breath and counsel – and advice from the crowd which had gathered, behind the safety of garden walls, to watch our efforts with calm, analytical criticism. Stone was terse with one old lady who said it was a shame to goad the poor animal so, it was obviously tired. Patch sat down, tongue lolling, alert for our next move. A boy came by on a bicycle with the cheering information that that big red cow of ours was in Black's stackyard, and 'the little white 'un wasn't 'alf making a mess of Mrs Storm's laylock.'

Stone and I decided the bull could well stay where he was while we rounded up the rest of the herd and fetched them back, and then we should have to take a chance on it and force the bull through the one small bit of hedge which formed part of the boundary of his self-chosen pen.

And then reinforcements arrived. Patch leaped to his feet as the Red Devil and the little white heifer came trotting down the road, the Master behind them on his ramshackle bike and Lass flying beside him. Stone and I gave a shout of welcome and suddenly the situation completely changed. No longer were we outwitted and outmanoeuvred. We had a man and a dog to spare, and the bull knew it. He lowered his broad head and walked through the thickset hedge as you or I would walk through meadow grass, shook himself, and set off peacefully along the road between the two cows.

The rest was plain sailing and it was just ten o'clock as we drove our two cows and the visitor through the yard gates and shut them thankfully. He was to stay with us for about a month. I stood and watched him for a moment before we went across to the dug-out. He was a lovely fellow, broad of forehead and shoulder, slender of hip, his serious eyes set deep in whorls of fur rather like the eyes of a toy animal. He looked up at me contemplatively, as though he were already making his plans for the return journey. I found myself inclined to agree with him that it is better to travel hopefully than to arrive and that gateways should be regarded rather as invitations than as barriers.

Despite the exasperations and the sweat of these recurrent bridal marches, they do break the monotony, and it begins to look as though there will not be very many more of them. A pioneer in the village decided to give artificial insemination a trial last year, and in due course the local Cattle Breeders' Association representative attended.

Village opinion was very mixed but those who approved were in the minority. For a few weeks the topic was to the fore at any village gathering. I went down to The Plough for some cigarettes one night and listened over my shoulder while I was waiting for my change.

'No, I don't 'old with un,' Bob was saying. 'That's going agin nature, come what may, it can't lead to no good.'

'They bin doing it in Roosia these many years, Em were telling me,' said George.

'Roosia!' said Bob, drawing viciously at his cigarette. 'They may be good at fighting and I'll give 'em credit where it's due, but what do we know they knows about farming? Old bull's bin good enough for us up to now, why do we want to go traipsing about after new ideas like this'n for?'

Bob's views are, however, suspect. Bob is stockman at the only farm where a bull is kept in the village and Bob collects his modest rake-off on every service to neighbours' cows. Someone else – I think it was Charlie – carried the conversation a stage further by wondering how long it would be before they tried it on human beings too, but there I got my change and left them to it, which was possibly just as well, knowing a little of the line such conversations are apt to take.

I think everyone was astonished when it became evident that Ernie's cow really was in calf by the strange new process; somehow they had never really believed it would work. As her time drew near, interest became intense and never had Ernie's cowman been so popular. He was taciturn, however, taking the line that seeing is believing, and the doubting Thomases must wait.

And then, one Sunday morning of course, the event came off and by dinnertime everyone had heard that Ernie had got his 'artificial calf' and that it was said to be a fine little heifer with a lovely head on her, and mother and daughter both doing well.

It was nearly a week before I had a chance to go and see the little beast. It certainly was a little beauty and although I shall never be an expert on such matters, I could agree with the good points in her as Ernie pointed them out. He took me indoors to show me the certificate, with the name of the bull, and I stayed talking a minute.

'Well, you've given the critics the lie, anyway,' I said.

He laughed. 'Yes, I think we have. It's really been very funny, you know. I think everyone's been down to have a look at her. Old Kennet, now. You know what a dry old stick he is. He came along to ask if he could see her and I'll swear he expected to see something with only three legs or two tails! He just stood and peered in over the door and said "Well I'll be beggared, now!" And then Stone –'

'Did Stone come down?' I said. 'He never told me!'

'Oh yes, he came all right,' said Ernie. 'He stepped inside the place without a word, his cap tilted down over his nose – you know. And there he stood a full minute before he said "Ah! Ah! Well, now!"'

The excitement died down a bit after that, but three other farmers took to artificial insemination, including my own. Village opinion in general went in favour too, particularly among the luckless juniors who had the unenviable task of driving cows over to the bull, with all that it entailed of blood and tears and toil and sweat, chasing recalcitrant animals out of front gardens, back yards, side lanes and what not. Young Johnnie voiced the feelings of us all, I think, when he said, 'It may cost a bit more this new way, but I'd willingly pay that out of my own pocket to be shut of that ruddy awful job! You get all of a muck sweat, and then chilled; many's the cold I've taken after it.' The only real critic left in the village seemed to be Bob: he's losing all his customers one by one.

*The Master, Stone and Beauty getting straw for a stack bottom.*

# THE HARDEST JOB OF ALL

For two months – with intermittent breaks on account of bad weather – we were threshing, and we had the help of six Italian prisoners of war. At first there was a very natural atmosphere of armed neutrality on both sides; we were unconsciously thinking of uncles, brothers, friends still out in North Africa; they were remembering their comrades – we were both remembering we were enemies. Gradually the mere fact of working together through the exigencies of the day's demands began to thaw us out. One of the men made a sparrow trap with three little slips of wood and a bit of board. David and I went and examined it, drew Stone's attention to it. Grudgingly he came to have a look at it, stared a moment, then smiled. 'Cor,' he said, 'I'm made 'undreds of them time I wer a boy,' and indeed I discovered all the village boys know the trap very well. Differ the ways of countries never so much in their more sophisticated aspects, in these simple things there is a common denominator, which gives one hope that the day may come when war between the peoples of different nations will be as unthinkable as war would be nowadays between, say, Yorkshire and Lancashire.

Apparently the gangs of prisoners were sent out in alphabetical order; the surnames of all our men began with a P. They were not, therefore, all from the same unit. Two were from the crack Bersaglieri regiment, now armoured: one was an artilleryman, from a mountain unit operating on skis; the other three were infantrymen, from different regiments. They were all captured in the first few days of our advance from El Alamein, and they were all unreservedly glad to be out of the war.

Our first efforts at conversation were single words about the work. None of them spoke any English, except a hesitating 'Good morning!' and none of us had a word of Italian, except odd words from musical scores, or the titles of operas, and somehow I did not quite see how I could work in such things as 'La donna e mobile', particularly as our old mare is anything but! I had hoped one of them might speak French, but we were unlucky. Nevertheless, I found my rusty French was a bit of a help, backed up by even rustier Latin, most of it ecclesiastical, and one of the men had a tiny dictionary which helped us over the worst patches. After a day or two we had exchanged the words for the job in hand – oats, barley, wheat, chaff, sack, hay, fork, straw and the like – and even managed to pick up bits of information about each other. And somehow one feels more human when names have been exchanged and one can call a man 'Carlo' instead of plucking him by the sleeve.

Carlo was the first of them with whom I exchanged words. He told me he came from El Alamein, was an artilleryman in a ski unit, that his home was in a little Lombardy hill village where he helped on a family farm, that after the war he intended to go to join an uncle in America, that his mother was displeased with him for allowing himself to be taken prisoner, and that his father was English! Carlo was short, thick-set, dark-haired, blue-eyed, slow to speak and yet his English was soon better than any of the others. The others were content to rub along with a minimum of nouns, but Carlo painstakingly filled in his gaps with verbs and other parts of speech. It was Carlo who made the bird trap, borrowing my knife, his own having been confiscated when he was taken prisoner.

Giovanni was a shop assistant in Siena, a tall raw-boned fellow, fairhaired and with grey eyes. Giovanni was a fanatic, quick-tempered, yet good-natured and friendly as a small child. This was my first impression of him, and because of it I was a little alarmed when David one lunchtime actually dared to mention the war, and our continued successes in North Africa. Giovanni, squatting on his heels, looked at him earnestly. 'Victory Italy, good!' he said. 'Victory England, good. I no interest!' All he wanted, he explained, was 'Finish guerra, go 'ome.' And after lunch, as he worked beside me, he haltingly found words to tell me, driven home with gestures, how friends had been blown to pieces beside him, how one man had gone out of his mind. Giovanni had no use for Mussolini and indicated forcefully just what he would like to do to Il Duce should opportunity ever offer. It was for Giovanni I braided up straw in the various patterns Stone had taught me. He was delighted with the results and placed them carefully in his haversack, telling me he would take them back to their campo and put them in what he called the 'presepio'. This puzzled me, and finally I decided he meant some sort of museum they had got at their camp, but Christmas came soon after, and in comparing notes with them about customs in Italy and England, the word kept coming up, and at last I discovered its meaning: Giovanni was going to use my straw braids as part of the decoration of the manger they were making in the camp chapel.

In charge of the gang was a corporal-major, who wore two narrow chevrons and one broad one and apparently ranked between corporal and sergeant. He was a tall, dark fellow with aquiline features and a very mobile face. His boys did not seem to take his NCO-ship very seriously and sometimes his eyes flashed when they took their own line! He was an engineer before the war and his long slim fingers could turn themselves to anything. Giuseppe was quick to understand, but I have my suspicions that he was not averse to feigning non-comprehension on occasion.

There was another Giuseppe (we have told them the English equivalent is Joseph, the same as Stalin), a plump little fellow, the only one of the group to conform closely to the idea of a typical Italian. He might be an ice-cream merchant, but in actual fact was a master carpenter. A gay, friendly lad, very popular with his mates and tougher at work than his plumpness would lead one to think. He came from the Austrian borders of Italy and the others ragged him about his German dialect.

'Cookie' was a bit of an enigma and even his fellow-prisoners could not always understand what he said. Corporal-major said he spoke a dialect 'similar Scotch to English'. He was an agricultural worker, a tractor driver, and he went nearly wild with excitement when the Master let him start up the tractor and manoeuvre it about into position. After that he established himself as starter and general nurse to the Fordson. I have an idea he might prove a rather irresponsible tractor man, with little care whether he landed in a ditch or not, but certainly he was happy seated on the beloved 'macchina'. From eleven o'clock till one 'Cookie' tended a stick fire, and hung a gigantic cauldron over it to make coffee, while he fried bacon, eggs, sausages or whatnot ready for his mates, and at one o'clock before we made for home and dinner he always called out 'Mees! Coffee?' and handed me a bowl of scalding hot coffee before passing it to Stone and David. Lovely coffee, too, good flavour with plenty of milk and sugar in it. At first Stone was sceptical of 'furrin stuff', and took a sip only for politeness; later he lapped up his share with avidity.

Finally there was the handsome man of the party; small though he was, he had a lovely build and carriage. Anselmo was one of the two Bersaglieri men; their comrades call them 'Gallena', or the Chickens, from their cock's tail peacetime headdress. Anselmo was fiercely proud of his regiment, and had managed to save the two bronze stars and tiny coloured flashes they wear on their collars, and had sewn them on to the collar of his brown-dyed battledress. It was Anselmo who marched briskly up and down, pitchfork to represent rifle, as the corporal-major yelled barrack-square instructions to him, and his precision of movement was a joy to watch. Gone for a moment the rather shambling gait imposed by ill-fitting clothes of alien cut, gone the mud and muck of the farmyard, and for a moment one saw again the smartness of a crack soldier carrying out orders like a lovely piece of machinery – a lovely piece of machinery dragooned into an evil scheme bent only on wreckage and destruction.

This was our gang, and they worked well, cheerfully, and happily with us. A lorry brought them at half-past eight each morning, called for them at half-past four – a lorry full of shouting, gesticulating boys who might be out on a school treat. Their company certainly enlivened one of our hardest jobs of the year. And now we have finished threshing, and they will not be driving up noisily to the yard each morning, filling the lane with snatches of song, wild jokes and laughter.

When the prisoners piled into their lorry already nearly full of chattering, gesticulating fellow-prisoners, I did not say a final 'Goodbye' to them because I had an idea we should be seeing them again – either the six we had got to know, or some of their fellows – and there had even been sporadic talk of having one or two living at the farm and working as permanent members of the staff, but I did not envisage quite what was going to happen as far as I was concerned.

It was just about four o'clock on a Friday afternoon when the big canvas-roofed lorry drove out of the yard. At five minutes to five the Master came across from the house, his wallet in his hand, to pay us. We usually end the day as we begin it, in the stable, and it is there he comes to hand us each our money, but tonight he called me out to him and as I went a sudden premonition flashed into my mind. With my money he handed me a little folded paper with my name on it. I knew at once what it contained, from his rather awkward manner. I opened it in front of him as we stood there. It gave me one week's notice.

They say just before you die your memory does a flashback over your past life. I don't know yet how that may be; I only know as I stood there I suddenly saw again the innumerable calves who had learned to drink with my finger in their clamorous mouths in the warm milk: I felt them at my knees with their seeking damp muzzles, saw their tails swing and twitch happily as the warm drink ran down their throats. I saw the hens come running to meet me over the snow, or more leisurely in the glare of an August afternoon; saw the eager heads dipping and rising from the water trough into which I had just emptied a pail of clean, cool water. I remembered the bitter winter weather of 1941–2 in particular when, the Master being laid up in hospital, on me had fallen all the milking, after lighting the copper fire and putting out the cows' breakfast, the hurricane lamp giving up its dim warm light from the cow lodge table, the cow lodge my special province that I kept always sweet and clean with fresh straw and new whitewash. I saw again the place next to the cow lodge, that we call the Maternity Home, saw it particularly as I saw it when I looked over the half-door, swinging my lamp shoulder-high and found not the cumbrous, puzzled Red Devil of the last week or two, but a slim, almost youthful figure nuzzling a still damp very curly-haired little son less than an hour old and tottery on his spindly legs. I went in and patted them both, then fetched the pail and milked the thick yellow 'beastings' from her while she stood as good as gold, turning her head from time to time to lick her son. I remembered, too, how my little white heifer became the mother of a lovely roan daughter, Christiansand, less than a month later, how I had rubbed her down with a wisp of dry straw and tidied up after her arrival. I saw again the calf that went down with scour. The Master had merely shrugged his shoulders when Stone and I had suggested the vet and it was I who brought the ground ginger from my kitchen store cupboard, and Stone and I who went back to the farm on a Saturday and Sunday afternoon to dose the invalid. The calf pulled through and when it was on its feet again the Master regarded it one day rather shamefacedly over the fence. 'You're better farmers than I am,' he said shortly as he turned away.

One of the reasons given for my dismissal was that I was unreliable with stock. I felt the matter was, well, open to argument.

The second reason given was that there was a lot of hard work in front of them, where I should not be suitable to fit in. Hard work? Is there any farm work that is not hard work? And there had not been a job going on the farm during the three-and-a-half years I had worked there, in which I had not taken my part; never a job I had refused to do, though I discovered afterwards, more than once, that I had been half-expected to; never the roughest day when I had baulked at the weather. My memory was working again.

I saw the harvest fields ripe for cutting and Stone bent before me, swinging his scythe, the corn falling before him. It was my job to follow swiftly after him, gathering the corn into sheaves and tying it with swathes. After an hour I thought there was no room for another thistle in arms or hands, but there always was room, and the job went on from the dewy early hours of double summertime morning to the still hot evening. And no sooner was the binder over the field than we went shocking, then pitching and stacking and threshing and chaff-cutting. Dawn to dusk, dawn to dusk, day after day, week after week, so that I hardly saw my own home in daylight save to snatch food, and when I went home at night I fell into bed and was asleep as my head touched the pillow.

Is harvest time more or less hard work than winter? It is difficult to say, it is all unremitting, though perhaps in summer it is more high-speed, working against time and weather.

I thought of tractor-driving on cold, raw November mornings when I could not see from end to end of the field for mist, while all day I was alone save for the wheeling, crying plovers. I thought of standing in six inches of near-freezing water, while I trimmed a neglected hedge and ditch; thought of two solid months of shifting tons of stubborn grey clay when we were draining a sodden bit of land.

Hard work! As I walked home across the footpath for the last time the sinking February sun cast a long-legged skinny shadow before me. I used to weigh ten-and-a-half stone, now I scale only just over eight, but I suppose it wasn't hard work that lost me those two stone. I looked down at my hands, rough, calloused, grimed beyond hope, nails trimmed to the quick. More soft living! By then I knew I was angry, almost more angry than hurt, too angry to be able to face working out my week's notice, cost what it might. You see, I knew the other reason, the one that wasn't in the note: four Italian prisoners were taking up residence at the farm the following week.

Two hours after the Master handed me my notice – as soon, in fact, as I had had my tea and cleaned myself up a bit – I got another job on a farm close to home and I started there on the following Monday. (I heard, later, that the Master was wroth that I had not worked out my notice, that he threatened to come after me for a week's wages, that Stone had argued, 'Ah, Master, let a dead dog lie. . .' Anyway, I heard nothing).

I felt rather like a new boy in the first days of his first term at a new school. I felt lost, in strange surroundings, amongst strange mates. I missed Stone. It was worse, oddly enough, than changing from office life to farm work. Ah well – the job changes, but the work goes on.

My way to work no longer lay across the field footpath beside the hedge. Instead, I turned to the right as I left my gate, went down past the pump and the little whitewashed school, round the corner short of the rather attractive little cluster of cottages with pantiled mansard roofs that make them look almost Dutch, and along the lane with the church tower before me. My own little watercress stream that passes the house went with me all the way, crystal-clear and bubbling happily. The farm lay at the end of the lane, just on the left, and the church and its neat little churchyard were almost part of the farm buildings; we used the footpath through the churchyard as a shortcut. The house was an attractive place, nearly all its windows facing south or east, cream-washed walls, ruddy lichened roof. In front, a patch of lawn surrounded by borders, and shaded by two huge conifers. The buildings lay in the usual rough square round the yards. The stable which was once a barn was so old it was mentioned in the local guidebooks, and the barn which was still used as a barn was as lofty and austerely cool and friendly as barns always are, the great solid timbers running up into the dim springing arches of the roof. On a blustery winter day I have been in that barn and watched the whole fabric shudder and sway under the sudden blast of a gigantic blow from the wind, yet still it stands as it has stood for so long. There were the usual piggeries, converted into hen-houses, and smaller barns, a handy workshop with the usual confusion of tools for repair, under repair and beyond repair, two chaff places, a small granary, a cow lodge ... but not my old beloved cow lodge with its deep thatched roof and one small door. This new cow lodge was only an open-fronted shed with a manger along the back wall and chains to tether the cows for milking. I struck mild winters while I was there, and I never knew what it was to sit there with the snow piling in on me, but I can imagine it. In the heat of summer, though, it was cool enough.

I took a long time to get over the pangs of being a 'new boy'. I should think for more than a month I was at a loss, lonely, and unhappy. I missed Stone and David, missed the routine I had grown to know, the fields I knew and loved, the implements and their idiosyncrasies. I went from one job to another on tenterhooks, feeling my way, wondering if I was doing the right thing. The work, too, was new to me, rather to my astonishment. This was a bigger farm than the other one, nearly twice as big, and we went in less for the wheat and corn crops that are general round here, more for cash crops like Brussels sprouts, sugarbeet seed, wurzel seed. For the first six weeks, bar odd half-hours looking after cattle, straw carting and so on, I think my back was never straight. First I was bent nearly double picking sprouts, and those were days of rain and blasting cold east and north-east winds, so that we went about with sacks tied round our bodies, heads down, fingers numbed and wet. I was unmitigatedly miserable for a day or two, till I learned the how of it a bit, made myself a pair of armlets out of an old oilskin, and found out how best to tie two small sacks round my thighs to stop the worst of a soaking from the wet Brussels plants. At my other farm we jacked up and found indoor jobs on wet days; here there were more of us, and fewer indoor jobs, so that we just went on. Even on days when blinding showers of almost horizontal rain forced a halt of a few minutes every now and then. During one such shower I was struck with the appearance of my mates. Each had a sack tied around his waist like a skirt, another over his head, coal-heaver fashion, each stood back to the driving rain, arms folded, hands tucked up sleeves, and because there was nothing to be said, all stood in silence. I wished I were an artist, to paint that rural Angelus.

Then came a break in Brussels picking. The young sugarbeet plants huddled in their seedbed were crying out for room, and the weather had made the soil warm and friendly for them. The rest of the gang went up the distant field which had already been marked out crisscross with lines twenty-eight inches apart, and I was sent to pull plants to keep them supplied. I had nearly three weeks of that, and most of it completely alone. If Brusselling had meant being bent nearly double, plant pulling meant a stoop of another six inches, and a heaving and pulling with both hands on top of it; the ground was solid, the plants abnormally big after a mild winter. I suppose the seedbed covered about three acres; I only know it seemed that in comparison Hercules had an easy time of it, and that each day I felt my legs must be getting shorter, telescoping under the continual pulling and heaving! Just to show me there were still bits of me to ache, I had a couple of odd days plant-setting till my right wrist swelled and ached with the thrust and tapping home and my back still had no chance to straighten itself. The planting caught up on the pulling and back I went to pulling. Somehow the acres were gradually filled with neatly spaced plants, temporarily wilted and unhappy till their young roots sent out fresh whiskers, and then we all went back to the Brussels, to find the stems bushy with 'blowers', and the neat tight tops open and yellowing. Whereas before it had taken us about two hours to work across the field we now covered it in just under an hour, picking only the best. And this time we picked straight for market, two of the team carrying spring balances from their belts, instead of picking full bags, shooting them up at the farm, picking them over and removing yellow leaves and other defective sprouts. There was the inevitable 'boy' among our team, a raw youngster with a surprising heart of gold and a way with children and young animals. He seldom elected to appear on Saturday mornings, and if he did then it took him all Monday to recover from the shock, so on Saturday mornings it fell to me to take the loaded sprouts to the station a couple of miles away. New implements, new horses. I had a luxurious but distinctly un-weatherworthy four-wheeled trolley, and Daisy who knew her way better than I did, but made her own pace – a sullen joggle on the way out, a racey turn of speed coming home! I enjoyed the expedition, for the novelty of it, but the road was hedgeless most of the way and the east wind cut across the flat country murderously and I was paralysed by the time I got to the station yard. Somehow I managed to throw off the sacks in which I had tried to protect myself, staggered off the trolley, and stumped my way to the platform. It is a one-eyed little station on a branch line, and the porter is also signalman and ticket-collector. As it happened, he was signalman when I arrived and he invited me into his box to have a warm up. Two trains were due (the event of his day) and he could not see to me for ten minutes. I began to thaw out enough to take an interest in his levers and telephones and bells and charts and books, and by the time we had exchanged cigarettes, and unloaded my ton of sprouts into a waiting truck in the siding, I was more or less humanly mobile and able to face the journey back. Daisy, who had not been in the signal box, was glad to be on the move, and facing homewards, and we got back before I had time to get really chilled again.

When the sprouts had been picked over for the last time, the boy and I had a lively two days slashing the tops off to within about six inches of the ground, preparatory to their being ploughed in. We raced along the rows, taking two each, slashing left and right with our bagging hooks, the heavy-foliaged tops going down before our onslaught like live things. After a raw misty start, the sun came out, and we shed our jackets. Then we shed sweaters, then overalls and caps, till we received admonitions in mock alarm from the rest of the gang, still picking on the further side of the field! We yelled ribaldry back at them and went on with our slashing.

There were Italian prisoners at my second farm too, five of them, all from the Italian working class (all from Sicily as it happened), and I had all over again the fun of hearing them learn the rudiments of conversation in English. None of them possessed a word of any language other than their own, unless you count 'OK!' and 'San fairy ann!' and amongst our resident team besides myself with a rusty residue of Latin and a creaking skeleton of school French, only the Boss admitted even to the existence of other tongues, and his French was rather more sketchy than mine! The rest of our workers took the line voiced by one of them when he said, 'Ruddy awkward beggars, what do they want to talk like that for? I suppose it means something to them, but if they want me to understand them they'll have to learn to talk English!'

Yet after about six weeks there was nothing we could not manage to convey to each other and at times I have plunged into quite abstruse discussions on politics, philosophy, sociology and other fundamentals. How did it come about? We invented our own international language. It started, of course, with nods and shakings of the head, beckonings, pointings and example, and they found I could pick out words here and there because of my meagre Latin and French. Curiosity pushed us a little further. Like children, we pointed and said the name of the object in our own language, and they replied with their word. Before long we built up a skeleton vocabulary for implements and jobs, for items of food and clothes, for essential verbs. Not all the words were English. For quite unaccountable reasons, certain Italian words caught on with us and now we use them even among ourselves in place of the English equivalents. 'Possibile', 'avanti', 'indietro' are three, while 'similar' has almost completely ousted 'like'.

It was amazing how few words were found necessary to say almost anything. Amazing how one word could be stretched to do the work of half a dozen. Our most popular verb was 'speak' which did service for 'say', 'tell' and 'ask' so that 'Boss speak me, I speak you, speak Stan take cart in field,' meant 'The boss said I was to tell you to ask Stan to take a cart down to the field.' Prepositions were simplified; 'in' worked overtime and was used for 'at' and 'to' as well. Thus 'I go in farm' meant 'I am going to the farm.' The present tense, it will have been gathered, did duty for all tenses; for the past we merely brought in a word like 'yesterday' or 'this morning'; for the future, 'tomorrow' or 'after mangiare', 'mangiare' being one of the words we adopted from Italian since it served to cover all the meals of the day! Auxiliary verbs were cut out, questions indicated solely by intonation, aided sometimes by a raised eyebrow. Definite and indefinite articles we ignored. I have already said we adopted the word 'possibile' but its meaning was not limited to 'possible' or even 'possible'; it also stood for 'perhaps', 'maybe', 'can you?', 'I might be able to'. For instance, 'Possibile I come in farm after mangiare five o'clock,' could mean, 'I might be able to come to the farm after tea.'

Of course some of the precise meaning was indicated by the circumstances of the moment and probabilities known to all of us. Sometimes finer shades of meaning were lost and things went a bit wrong. I remember Salvatore coming to me one day with a message from our foreman, 'Stan speak you put cows in field.' As I had already turned them out in the meadow as usual immediately after milking and could see them grazing quietly, I decided to ignore the message till a small boy came to tell me one of our heifers had got through the hedge into our neighbour's kale and would I kindly drive it home! If the matter were really serious, however, we took pains to see that we were understood. For the rest, misconceptions gave us quite a lot of fun and quite a lot of loopholes, on both sides, for interpretations to suit our own wishes!

Expressions foreign to all of us were interesting. I have mentioned 'OK' and 'San fairy ann' but to the Italians the latter evidently meant something more sinister than the shrug of the shoulders for which it stood in our eyes. They seemed quite shocked when I repeated it after them one day, and refused to explain what it meant to them. I had my own idea, later, based on hints dropped by one of our boys who wormed some sort of explanation out of Angelo but they always wilted a bit when we used it, though they soon realised how innocuous it was for us. In this connection, inevitably they picked up some dubious expressions from us and we have collected a pithy set of phrases which will probably be best forgotten if ever any of us goes to Italy. Someone is going to have a puzzle in years to come when he hears the oldest inhabitant giving vent to a fluent string of Sicilian oaths over the pint pot! Another international word is 'compris' and its negative counterpart. It was a long time before I realised the Italian for 'understand' was 'capisce' whereas they seemed to think 'compris' was good Anglo-Saxon.

Finally we built the beginnings of idiom in our pidgin-Italo-English. For some unknown reason we never said 'I come back' but 'I come in back,' and other similar curiosities gradually grew up.

It was all very amusing and instructive. I can't see that it led anywhere except to enable our gang to work conveniently together. It even got in the way of one or two of us, in both camps, who wanted to make some attempt to learn the other language properly. We had got so used to the bastard version that it was impossible to get out of the bad habits formed! As a pointer, it had its lesson. We shall have to find an international language before civilisation gets very much older. In fact, unless we do I'm not sure that it will get very much older.

I was looking through the local paper one night and sooner or later turned, as I always do with country papers, to the notices of farm sales. Not so many these days, and not much to be picked up in the way of bargains. Agricultural implements, machinery and tools are fetching their pre-war new values if they are serviceable at all.

Looking through those advertisements, my mind went back to my first agricultural sale, a few months after I started farm work. It was in my own village, in the stackyard right under my bedroom window. My neighbour was moving from the district and selling off his livestock and much of his dead stock too. Not only that, but various neighbours took advantage of the sale to push in a few items of their own so that before the catalogues were out everyone in the village seemed to have something at stake.

The Master was very deeply concerned. Not only had he taken the chance to dispose of two pensioned pony traps, but two of our horses were in the list. I say 'our' but the position was a bit complicated. Another neighbour had gradually sold his substance to keep himself going. Only a few fields remained, one wagon, a tractor, and two horses, Short and Turpin. He had nowhere to house them, nothing on which to feed them and little use for them so we stabled and fed and cared for them and had their work in return, and the arrangement had gone on for so long that we regarded them as our own. Then the blow fell. He came to us one day and explained that they would have to go. Would we please groom them and take them over for the sale? Consternation fell on us. Stone's moustache bristled more than usual as he angrily brushed them down that night. The Master wandered about, brow wrinkled, as he puzzled out ways and means. 'Stone,' he said at last, 'we can't run to both of them. Which is it to be?' – Stone looked up under the peak of his cap. 'There ain't no two thoughts to it, master,' he said. 'Short's bin a good un but now 'e ain't got no pluck to 'im. 'E starts off full o' beans, but the 'eart goes out of 'im in 'alf an hour. You git Turpin if you can. 'E'll go all day and keep going.'

We got through our routine jobs next morning as quickly as possible. Stone gave the horses an extra grooming and then he and I went home to clean ourselves up a bit. I pondered, not knowing quite what was expected of me. Finally I decked myself out in the full glory of my best set of uniform, hat, armlet and all, and gave my wellingtons a wash at the sink. As I went back, I met Stone at the handgate, wearing his best winter overcoat with the velvet collar. 'Good gal!' he said, and I knew I had done the right thing.

Bidding at auctions is one of the major mysteries of life to me still. Not a word is spoken to interrupt the steady monologue of the auctioneer, yet steadily the prices mount. 'Now then, gentlemen, what am I bid for this in-calf heifer? A nice useful animal. Thank you, sir. Ten pounds from this gentleman for a start. Eleven, thank you. Twelve. Twelve I'm bid. Thirteen, thank you. Thirteen. I'll take the half. Thirteen-ten. Fourteen.' And so it goes on till the hammer finally falls and not a word from the audience! Listening won't help you. Watch, very carefully. A nod here, a finger raised there, a shake of the head, a catalogue flicked. The auctioneer knows them all, knows who is likely to be bidding for each lot. I watched and listened, fascinated and bewildered, as lot after lot went by. It was a quarter to one and the cows had gone and the sow and her youngsters. 'And now, gentlemen, we'll take the horses if you please. Lot 16, chestnut gelding.'

Stone and I exchanged one frantic glance. Lot 16 was Turpin, they had changed the order of the sale and the Master was in another field, bent over a tangle of twisted steel hawser and chains which might be worth having. We tore away, making a concerted rush. Stone yelled incoherently but when Stone yells you can hear at least his voice for miles. The Master heard and came running. He arrived panting at the back of the ring which had been formed round Turpin who was being paced slowly up and down. 'I'm taking guineas, gentlemen. Fifteen guineas I'm bid, gentlemen. What rise on fifteen guineas?' I looked cautiously at the Master. His auburn-tinged curls jerked fiercely up, not a muscle moving on his face. 'Sixteen guineas I'm bid. What advance on sixteen guineas? Thank you, sir. Seventeen guineas – any advance on seventeen guineas?' Again the Master's head jerked up. 'Eighteen guineas, thank you. Eighteen. Any advance on eighteen? Any advance, gentlemen? Eighteen guineas I'm bid. Going at eighteen guineas.

Going, going, gone!' His little hammer fell, he nodded to the Master, made a note in his book and went on to the next item.

A long time ago now, that first sale of mine. The traps fetched precisely four and sixpence apiece and the Master laughed shortly when he got the money. They would have been worth more to us as firewood or in bits and pieces. Short went for fifteen guineas, but we were not interested. And now Turpin is dead, his day of hard and willing service ended. A lock of his tail hangs neatly plaited over my mantelpiece. But he had his hour, with the crowd round him and voices praising him and the Master buying him in with that sudden jerk of the head that was the highspot in the drama of my first farm sale.

We had acres and acres of sugarbeet to plant out, for seed. We had been at the job for three weeks on end and I began to think seriously of giving up sugar in my tea. When people tell me what a happy, healthy, carefree life one leads on the farm, I long to reach out and take them by the hair of their heads, put a dibber in their hands and let them loose to plant thirty acres of sugarbeet on a raw morning with a sharp northeaster cutting over the top of the close-trimmed hedges.

And then I got a break. As I took the milk into the kitchen I ran into the Boss. 'Oh I want you to take Pet and a cart and go and fetch that wheel from Grave's and while you're at it you'd better take the old blue ladder and let him put a new side on it. If you haven't got any dinner with you, nip home and get some. Peter can get the old mare ready while you're gone.'

As I cut across the orchard and up through the bottom of my garden my heart was bounding with thankfulness. By the time I got back the day would be so near finished it would not be worth while going right down to the sugarbeet field. For one day my dibber would lie wrapped in its bit of bag under the hedge; maybe it would be as glad of the break as I was. I tore into the house, seized half a loaf and a hunk of cheese and a couple of apples and stuffed them into my dockey bag and was back by the time Peter had harnessed Pet and yoked her into the cart. I filled her nosebag and put it beside my oilskin, lashed the broken ladder firmly to the cart, clambered up, shook out the reins and set off. Grave's yard and workshop is in a village over the hill. It was a nice morning, but cold and I was glad to turn up the collar of my greatcoat and stick my hands in my pockets, reins linked over one arm. The first mile of the journey lay through the village, past the school, its playground still silent and deserted, past the pump and my cottage sitting snug and cosy under its thatch. Our willow tree had come on quite a lot: a stranger recently asked for our house and was directed to 'the one with the willer tree in front!'

I met the postman a little further on and stopped while he handed me up my letters. I always loved the arrival of the postman, even in London; now, when my post inward and outward must constitute quite fifty per cent of the postman's work, I enjoy it even more. Letters mean so much more these days. I tried to read my brother's airgraph but two corners had to be negotiated, and then there was the milk lorry to wait for at the crossroads. Mr Clement was taking down the shutters outside the shop as I passed and then I was out of the village and climbing the only hill for miles. Anyone will tell you that East Anglia is 'just a plain; flat as your hand' but it isn't. Try cycling for more than a mile or two in any direction. Not startling ups and downs such as I have known and loved in my own south country, but gently undulating all the time with here and there a real hill like this one to give the critics the lie.

The journey was uneventful for the next few miles and then I went through another village and past the mill, the big millstones propped against the wall like giant cheeses. Beyond, the road ran along a hollow and then over the bridge not yet swollen with winter rains. I had just crossed the bridge when I met a huge scarlet tractor driven by a stocky little girl in my own khaki and green uniform.

At last I reached my destination and found my way to Grave's shop. I had eaten my dockey en route, while Pet had a breather, but now it was nearly dinnertime as I drove into the yard and jumped down. Yes, our wheel was ready and could I possibly take Mr Elliot's too while I was there? I could, but might I leave Pet in the yard while I found somewhere to have my dinner? Certainly, and if I liked to have it in the woodworking shop, I was welcome. If there's one thing I love more than another it is to be in a woodworking shop, with the sweet scent of wood on the air and curls and twirls of wood shavings all over the floor. I tied Pet to the fence, undid her bits and gave her her nosebag and went in and sat down to my dinner on a half-finished coffin – it made an excellent combination table and seat. As I brushed the last crumb to the ground, a small girl came out of the cottage with a steaming hot can of tea. 'Mummy thought perhaps you could be doing with a hot drink,' she explained. It was just what I wanted to finish off my snack meal and then I went out, well away from the wood, to have a cigarette.

Going back is never quite the adventure of setting out, but it was a nice ride home, with the sun and the wind behind me. Just before I got to the village I met the postman again cycling to our nearest station with His Majesty's Mail for the day. I reached the farm with only half an hour to spare and by the time I had unloaded and shut Pet out and unharnessed her and brushed her down, given her a drink and a sifting of oats, it was time to go and find my own tea. Johnnie on his bicycle overtook me as I neared my gate. 'Enjoyed your trip, mate?' he called.

'Rather!' I said. 'What have you been doing?'

'Planting sugarbeet,' said Johnnie disgustedly, and pedalled stiffly away up the road.

I had thought that farm work held no further terrors for me until the Boss said one evening, 'Oh I want you to go down to the Cattle Market tomorrow and fetch that reaper home.' Quite casually, like that, and he rode off on his bike. The Cattle Market is some eight miles away in our nearest town, and the trip therefore involved taking one of the horses in solo, going through the town to the Market, finding the reaper, yoking in and bringing the whole equipage back. I had never taken a horse into a town before; I hardly knew the horses on this farm yet.

The Boss said he'd do the milking next morning so I went straight into the stable to learn my fate. It was Daisy, and Ern had left her all ready dressed for me, with a fearsome array of spanners, hammers, wrenches and so on slung to her hame. The Boss came across as I led her from the stable. He gave me my final instructions, tossing a haphazard description of the reaper to me as I moved off. He thought it would have his name chalked on it somewhere. It was just half-past seven – half-past five by the sun – and I was glad of my pullover and the cover of my new dungarees. I had even dug out my Land Army hat for the expedition!

The first mile of the journey lay across home fields, along the footpath. It was very lovely and I sat back comfortably and enjoyed myself. I remember an old ambition to have a holiday on horseback, ambling through the lanes of Sussex. Then we came out on the main road and turned north. But Daisy wanted to go to the station; she always did go there when she came this way, and I had to argue with her a moment. She was obviously quite sure I had made a mistake. For the next mile she tried to go through every gateway or hedge opening or side turning. Then she gave up and let me have my way. By this time I wasn't so sure about that horseback holiday. Her spine seemed to be extraordinarily nobbly, even through two sacks flung across her back, and she was so wide that my legs wouldn't hang down properly.

The children were running across the green to school as I passed through the last village. Only a couple of miles now before we came to the outer suburbs. Daisy seemed quite happy till we met the first manhole cover just as we came abreast of the outlying houses. She stopped, looked suspiciously down, did a coy side-step, pawing the ground a little, danced kittenishly round the manhole cover, and went on. About six yards further on we repeated this little ballet dance. I swore heartily and goaded her on with my heels drumming against her ribs. About twenty yards ahead a patch of gleaming wet shone on the tarmac, glistening in the sun. One of the waterboard men had been turning on a stopcock. Daisy stopped, looked, side-stepped, pawed, danced and finally sidled broadside on across the road towards the open yard gates of the 'Hat and Feathers'. Luckily there was no traffic about and I got her back on her own side of the road. Then we met a big double-decker bus head on. Daisy stopped dead. I decided I had better get down while the initiative remained in my hands and slithered ungracefully to the pavement, thankful there was no one close enough to hear the startled grunt forced from me as the pavement met me. I was aware that the sweat from the horse had left a damp, warm, but rapidly cooling patch where the saddle ought to have been. . .

The Cattle Market is a raucous, hideous place of unhappy animals and battling humanity on Mondays, but on Thursdays it is empty and deserted. No one questioned me as I pushed back the rolling gate and led Daisy through, no one came near me as I wandered between the empty pens to the open space where the implements are sold. I was starving, it was long past my dockey time, so I sat myself down on the cobbled stones beside the reaper chalked with the Boss's name and opened my haversack and poured myself out a cup of hot tea. Daisy stood more or less patiently beside me. Two minutes later two very elderly gentlemen materialised seemingly out of thin air, and ambled up. One was lean and lanky, the other short and tubby. We exchanged greetings. Could they help me yoke the old mare in? Yes, I thought perhaps they could. I set down my cup of tea carefully and five minutes later we had Daisy between the shafts, tying up sundry missing links with binder string. They made me get on with my lunch while the tubby gentleman took my oilcan and dosed every joint and bearing liberally. I felt in my pocket and extracted some small change and proffered it in recognition of their help.

'Oh no, we don't look for nothing from working folk, mate!' said the lean one.

I demurred.

'No, that's all right, mate,' said the tubby one, 'we looks to the bosses for that, don't you worry. Glad to 'elp.'

For the thousandth time I registered my conviction that to get on happily in this world you must have either £5,000 a year or thirty bob a week, and I think I prefer the latter; the service you get on that level is genuine.

The reaper was over seven yards long from front to rear. It might be easy enough to handle in a twenty-acre field but in town I'd rather drive a ten-ton truck any day. My first bad moment came as I left the Market by way of a steepish ramp giving straight on to the mainest of main roads. Daisy facing homeward would stop for nothing, not even a manhole cover. By some streak of luck a police inspector happened to dismount from his bike just at that corner. He saw me, guessed my problem, stopped the main-road traffic and waved me on. I saluted gratefully and turned for home.

We came back in style. As soon as we got out of the town, I clambered onto the bar of the reaper and rode, my toes just swinging clear of the ground. Daisy adopted a steady jog-trot, her tail swishing rhythmically. It was five minutes to one as I unyoked her, unhitched her broadrein and led her through the gate into the yard. By one o'clock she was in her cool, quiet stable enjoying her dinner in peace. As I jumped the ditch which takes me home by the back way, I found myself smiling. Another milestone safely passed: Daisy and I had been to town and back.

*Lull in the storm: the threshing tackle is oiled at dockey time.*

# HEYDAYS AND HAY

AT LAST CINDERELLA went to the Palace. Not in ball dress with slippers of glass, but in corduroy breeches, green jerseys and flat-heeled iron-tipped shoes. Her Majesty the Queen gave a party at Buckingham Palace for the Land Army's birthday. They chose one representative among the veterans in each county, and I was there.

We came from all over the country. Not very many of us, lost amongst the blues and khakis and greys of London, yet standing for the background of the whole effort of them all. Three hundred of us, representing the rest who would go on working till we got back. Saturday morning I wandered along Oxford Street, Regent Street, New Bond Street, doing a little desultory shopping but mostly looking, noticing, enjoying, regretting. Smiling at the willowherb flaunting its rosy flowers on the heaps of rubble that were once proud buildings, at the coltsfoot pushing its way between paving stones, the plantains against railings. If anyone had told me, four years earlier, that I should see red admiral butterflies in High Holborn, and the white trumpets of convolvulus scrambling in Soho, I should have thought them crazy. The war which had driven me into the country had also driven the country into the heart of London.

Two o'clock and the Admiralty Arch, the rendezvous for our East Anglian contingent. We walked up the Mall together, and found the Mall suddenly swarming with corduroy and green. Then the pavements in front of the Palace seething, the gravelled forecourt full of us, the sentries gravely coming to attention, the click of their heels drowned by the solid tramp of our iron-tipped shoes, their pale faces paler still against our ruddy tan. Across the forecourt, through the grim facade we had known since childhood and never expected to enter. Through another inner courtyard and then up a few shallow stairs to where two scarlet-coated, top-hatted gentlemen stood waiting to take our cards from us and let us in. As we left our hats in the vestibule – mercifully we were allowed to go bare-headed into the Palace – the Palace Home Guard string band was tuning up at one end of the gallery, prior to breaking into 'The Farmer's Boy'. Left and right ran wide tables with tea spread out.

They lined us up, county by county, in one of the stately rooms overlooking the gardens and gave us our final instructions. We fidgeted and chatted. Suddenly one last warning, the great folding doors opened, and the long snake began to creep forward. Through that room we went, across the corridor, through another room and more folding doors, and we were there. A naval officer stood by the doors taking our cards from us, passing them to a general who read each name and county aloud. Till that moment I had been a bit nervous, self-conscious, aware that my breeches were the usual two sizes on the large size, that my shoes squeaked. Then I heard the clipped voice announce, 'Miss Barraud, Huntingdonshire, Cambridgeshire and the Isle of Ely!' and found myself stepping forward to a very friendly, smiling lady who held out her hand to me, shook hands and waved me on to where her two daughters stood ready to shake my hand in turn.

It was all over in a moment, and we were out in the gallery again, chattering and laughing and making gratefully for the tea, the wafer sandwiches which it was so hard to pick up one at a time, we who were used to great doorsteps! It was great fun in the relaxation from that one tense moment. Everyone was talking at once and the Palace servants were smiling as they passed us cups of tea, handed bowls of sugar, jugs of milk. A medalled man stopped in front of me, holding out a casket of cigarettes, with a little lamp to light mine for me. I smiled at him, but my smile was really for my mates back in the hayfield. They had pulled my leg as I lit my teatime cigarette the night before.

'Won't get no fags in the Palace!' they chaffed.

'Won't I?' I retorted, 'The Queen's a lady and a lady would always offer a fag to her friends!' and I was right.

Then there was a stir at the far end of the gallery, and a murmur: 'The Queen has come in!' The crowd milled slowly that way and there she was, the Princesses close by, in the middle of us, laughing and talking informally, asking questions, praising and congratulating. She asked one girl what her work was.

'Tractor driver, Madam.'

'I should have known,' she said, 'you tractor drivers are all so bright-eyed!'

For an hour or more she was there amongst us till everyone had had a word with her and then we went out into the gardens, strolled down to the lake, sat about under the great trees. It was hot out there in the sun and we were in our winter breeches and our warm jerseys, our collars restrained by ceremonial ties. We met old friends, and made new ones and then as the sun began to drop down over the trees, we began to slip away.

Next day we were back at work all over the country. Tractors started up again, hoes were taken down from the tool shed, milking overalls reached from the peg, pitchforks at work in fresh fields. I drove Pet up to the quarry, sitting on the rave of the cart. Ern was horse-shoeing in the mangolds and pulled his horses to a standstill to ask how I had got on. Art was ploughing between the young fruit trees, Fred had already made his mark on the clover ley where I had left them working to go and clean myself up. It all seemed very far away, that short afternoon, that crowd of laughing girls tramping gaily through the Palace precincts, the smiling, friendly lady who shook hands with us and gave us tea and cigarettes. I expect the rest of them had to stand as I did, all the way home in the train, but they could afford to smile, as I did. Cinderella in corduroy breeches, green jersey and iron-tipped shoes had at last been to the Palace.

The poets may write about the fragrant season, and holidaymakers and children regard the hayfields as ideal places for picnics and frolics but the farmer and his men for the most part detest it more than any other job. Haywork goes with an unremitting intensity that does not belong even to harvesting. Harvest hangs out so long that delays due to bad weather are inevitable; except for intermittent bursts, harvest takes its time, but hay may be made or ruined in a day and not a moment must be lost.

Between nine and ten o'clock of an evening when the sun is at last beginning to lose its intensest heat as it moves westward and the birds are singing again from hedges and tree-tops, all over the country agricultural workers are going home to their supper, trudging stiff-limbed. Their day began fifteen or sixteen hours ago, the younger ones whistling, the older ones silent or exchanging quiet greetings with mates passed on the road. Everyone knows everyone. As babies they tumbled and played outside cottage doors, as children they went to school together. Master and man they have been together since birth and worked together and will go side by side till one by one they lay down their tools for the last time and are carried by the same mates to their last resting place beyond the church tower under the shadow of the stately chestnuts.

But that time is not yet come, and before the birds were properly awake, all over the country, carts were rumbling along roads and lanes, through narrow gateways, over rough tracks to the hayfields. Little engines were uncovered and the worst of the hay and dust wiped from them. Elevator cogs were greased, the twisted hay cut and torn away from the bearings. Tractors sputtered and hummed and clinked, forks were retrieved from safe hiding places in hedge bottoms, jackets and lunch bags were hung from bushes and the team moved out into the sun. If the field is far from home, the stack will be made in one corner, carts dispensed with and the hay brought to the foot of the elevator by tractor and hay-sweep – a great outstretched hand of wooden tines pushed forward by the machine and gathering up the small piles raked up by the boy with the horse-drag. Two or three men on the stack, two or three round the foot of the elevator to fork the billowing heaps on to the ceaselessly moving band. I am an old hand now. I know where the stuff will come easiest just by looking at it and nowadays it is rather cruel fun to watch the ineffectually heroic struggles of amateurs to tear forkfuls from the unyielding mass.

If the field lies nearer home, the hay will usually be carted to make a stack in the yard, or stored in a barn and then it is the turn of the horses. Machinery is ousted for a moment and the whole burden falls on man and beast as it has done immemorially. Only the stacker's job is unchanged. For the rest, instead of the fight to keep the elevator fed they have to load cart after cart, keep a steady stream of supplies moving from the field to the farm and a steady stream of empties the other way. You must know your horses, allow for Pet's unhurrying pace, Gypsy's sudden snatches and shyness at the least incline, Beauty's tossing head that may mean a freelance decision to move forward, Daisy's inclination to back if spoken to sharply. A day in the hayfield will teach you one horse from another more quickly than a month of staring at them. By the end of the day one is a friend for life, the other a constant worry and anxiety.

I hate loading, having no head for heights, particularly when the height is increasing and the stability decreasing in direct proportion. Pitching is harder work, but at least you remain on terra firma! Loading can be a leisurely job but at the end of the day, with ten minutes to go and two carts still to fill, it can speed up to a miracle of co-operative efficiency, with hardly a pause between the boy's cries of 'Hold ye!' as he leads the horse from one haycock to another – and woe betide him if he fails to shout the warning to the man on top!

Unloading is one of the easier jobs so long as the stack is below the level of the cart. After that it becomes a matter of passing every forkful up. There isn't a single job about the whole process that is unskilled – even the middleman on the stack can help or hinder the smooth running of the work by failing to cope with the hay passed up to him, while, as to the business of unloading, believe me, until you know how and why a cart is loaded as it is, you may tug your guts out trying to get the next forkful. It is a safe rule to tell a novice at the job that he is standing on the bit that comes next; ninety-nine times out of a hundred he is, no matter how tempting the outer edge may look! As the stack rises, at the point where the stacker begins to draw in for the roof slope he builds the stage-hole, a tiny space left in the edge of the stack, and in the stage-hole stands the man whose job it is to take each forkful from the unloader thereafter, and pass it up over his head to the man on top. I have spent many a whole day in the stage-hole and remain convinced that it is the toughest job of all. The stacker will leave as little room as he dare, because the stage-hole remains a weak spot for leakage later. So only the veriest foothold is left, and after that each course round goes behind the stage-hole, till the man there is completely hemmed in. There is no room to sit down a minute between loads as others can. There is no room to wield even a shortish fork easily, and load after load draws up alongside, thousands of forkfuls are passed up, caught and handed overhead till at last the stage-hole man is reaching full stretch. It can be sheer agony if the man on the cart or the man above fail to co-operate properly with the man in the stage-hole. Then there is a break in the through swing, every forkful has to be angled and wrestled for. An hour of this is torture, particularly with the sun blazing down, but given a good team the whole thing goes with beautiful precision, carried through with one unbroken swing from the moment when the unloader sticks his fork into the hay to the moment when the stacker puts it in exactly the right position on the stack. It is a lovely thing to watch a good team stacking, the lovelier the more you know the job.

So it goes on from dawn to dusk, all over the country. We had some amateur help from people staying at the farm. They helped us for an hour or so in the cool of one evening. They prodded and heaved and strained and sweated and I take my hat off to them for their well-meant effort. One of them said to me, smiling pleasantly, 'Who says women can't work?' I hope I smiled as pleasantly back, because she was putting her whole self almost literally into it, but I longed to say, 'You've been at it for an hour, we've been at it for fourteen already, and it was hot, you remember, earlier in the day. This breeze didn't get up till teatime. For you, this hour has been a strenuous highspot, for us it has been a fraction of the day's usual uncompromising fight. We were at it yesterday. We shall be at it tomorrow. We were at it last year and shall be at it next year. My mates have been at it since they could walk and will be at it till they can stand no longer. All over the country we shall be going to homes we have not seen since daylight. This is our daily bread – and yours.'

# STAR FOR MY WAGON

It was a biting cold day, with sleet driving sharply before a north-east wind, when I took my WLA proficiency test.

There were seven of us gathered in the courtyard of the Shire Hall by two o'clock and of the seven, four wore the scarlet armlet of the four-year veterans. We stamped about, trying to get some circulation back into our feet, and finally piled into the two little cars that were to take us out to the farm where the tests were being held. On the run over, I had wondered what they could give us to do on a day like this. There seemed little else but muck-carting. I was right, and never was I so glad to have a muck fork thrust into my hand. Those carts must have been filled in something like record time and then we had to lead the laden carts out of a rather tricky yard, along a quarter of a mile of main road, and up a cart track to a dung heap for unloading. Those who had not handled the horses for harnessing and yoking in had the job of leading them home, taking them out of the carts and putting them back in the stable. So much for the practical test. It may not sound much, but it included all sorts of possibilities for error and you could feel the critical eyes of the judges boring into you at every move. Then came the oral, when we had to sit in a canteen and go one at a time to another room for our questions.

I sat down opposite my two Torquemadas. Papers rustled a moment, then came the first question: 'Tell me what you know about the rotation of crops.' My mind flashed back to the big barn at the farm that morning, the whir of the root-cutter, the slivers and chips of white and gold mangolds falling into the old enamel bath and the Boss leaning against the doorpost.

'You know about rotation, don't you?' he asked. 'The main thing is no two white straw crops in succession.'

'Yes,' I said, 'roots one year, to clean the ground, then wheat, then beans or peas, then barley or oats, then roots again.'

Torquemada No. 1 nodded as the Boss had nodded and produced his next question. 'You've had a clover ley and the land is to be prepared for wheat. What processes of cultivation would you carry out?'

'First plough.'

'How deep?'

'Four inches,' I said and I could see again the curve of the wave of soil falling away behind me as 'my shining darlings' bit deep into the earth.

'When would you drill the wheat?'

'October or November, according to the weather and state of the soil.'

'How much to the acre?'

'Three to three-and-a-half bushels.'

'Oats? How much to the acre?'

I was stumped and thought frankness better policy than a guess. I said I had never drilled oats. Had I handled pigs? No, only in an emergency, if Stone were ill. All right then, in such an emergency what would I do? I couldn't resist saying 'Look at their ration books first!' which brought a laugh. 'Then I'd collect any housescraps, and mix them in with the meal, and water, to a fluid gruel.'

'How much to a feed?'

'I'd go by the size of the troughs, and if they cleared it all up give them a bit more next feed; if they left any, cut it down a bit.'

Apparently as a first-aid measure I was on the right lines; Torquemada No. 1 handed me over to No. 2. 'What signs of sickness would you look for in cattle?'

'Dry nose, cold ears, staring coat, dull eye and, of course, listlessness, loss of appetite and any specific signs such as wounds, ringworm and so on.'

'Yes, and if the boss told you a certain animal had seemed off-colour and told you to go and look at it and report, and you found it lying chewing the cud what would you say?'

'That there wasn't much wrong with it!'

'Quite right. Appetite, and if a beast stretches when it gets up, are two pretty reliable signs.' Then they let me go.

We none of us got the same questions. We were all impressed with the practicability of what we were asked and the thoroughness. We felt we were having a fair deal and because that was all we asked, we were enjoying it. We enjoyed it too when a door suddenly opened and they brought tea in to us, and over tea we thawed out and began to talk, comparing notes about work and billets and what we had done before the war and what we wanted to do after it. For that short half-hour we were happily conscious of being members of a corporate body. That's something people are apt to forget about the Land Army; most of us are isolated commandos with no corporate life as the other forces know it. When the last girl came from the examination room she said, 'If we wait five minutes they'll tell us the results.' We had not hoped to know our fate so soon, so we poured out another round of tea and went on talking. The door opened and the two inquisitors looked in on us. Dead silence. No. 1 looked round the table. 'Well, you've all passed, I'm glad to say, and you' – nodding to the girl at one end of the table – 'have got distinction. You did well, even if one or two of you knew things we didn't expect you to know, and slipped up on things everyone ought to know! Congratulations all round!' Babel broke out for a few minutes and then we pushed back our chairs on the concrete floor, reached down our hats and greatcoats from the pegs, and made for the cars in the yard. Another milestone passed. In a week or two, we were promised, there would be a little gathering to give us our badges. Next time you see a Land Girl wearing a bronze star in her buttonhole, you'll know what it means. These tests are not exhaustive, they can't be in the time, but they do provide some sort of nationwide standard of general efficiency and as such are useful. As the Chairman of the County War Agricultural Executive Committee said at that 'little gathering' a few weeks later, 'Those of you who have won these stars have earned them, but don't run away with the idea that you now know everything!'

Stone put it rather more tersely: 'Ah gal,' he said, 'I'm glad you got it, but you needn't think chucking a bit o' muck into a cart and answering one or two ruddy questions and taking tea with your mates makes you fit to run a farm!'

It was five years before I had a holiday in the country. Such leave as I had had, never more than a few days at a time, had always been spent in rush trips to London and I looked at the country only from the windows of the train as we rushed through.

Then I had to go across country to keep an appointment about some literary work. The journey was only about fifty miles. I left the house at half-past seven in the morning and got back at half-past nine at night. I had precisely three hours at my journey's end! Yet there are still people who travel for pleasure in wartime!

But I was not concerned so much with the journeying as such. I was even glad of the long-drawn-out cross-country rambling voyage, of the lift on the lorry going into town, of the halting train journey from one small one-horse station to another, of the two hours' wait at one change, of the wrong train which flung me out at a tiny halt nakedly set along the line with not even a cottage to keep it company, of the two-and-a-half hours at another junction, of the tramp up a steep hill against time to try and hitch-hike twelve miles to link up again with the right train. It all made the day spread out till it became a real break and gave me a chance to look at the country close up.

Very different country from my own, too. Ours is heavy, stiff chalky clay, a sodden quagmire in winter, a dazzling barren-looking thing in summer, for all we grow fine wheat with its roots deep in the moisture while the sun beats richly down from our wide skies. Almost the first thing I noticed, as I looked out from the train while we ran along a steep embankment, was the stones lying on the surface of the reddish gravelly soil. Such big fields too. I am still not much judge of acreages at sight, but mentally I fitted three or four of Church Field into the fields below me and guessed some of them must run to thirty or forty acres. 'Moles!' I said to myself, noting the crazy weals running across the face of arable and pasture alike, with here and there a hummock thrown

Then there were trees. Not clumps and isolated elm, oak or ash, but roadside plantations, succulent-looking copses and real big woods such as I have known and loved in Surrey and Sussex and Kent. Such hilly country too, after my own flat landscape. Oh I know I defend Cambridgeshire and certainly it is nothing like the billiard table unkind critics would have it, but we have nothing like this, yet Suffolk is accounted flat.

I saw clover growing and noted the same unevenness of plant that we had at home, the result of last year's dry spell just when the seed had been drilled. Then another strange sight, a field of grain on the ear! The bearded ears waved silkily in the breeze. Rye! We never see rye our way but it could be nothing else as forward so early in the year. The first windmill held out its arms to me. I hadn't seen a windmill since, oh the derelict one at Peasmarsh, in Sussex, and that must have been on Christmas Day in 1938. We rambled past an aerodrome close to the line, with the giant Forts lined up round the perimeter, some camouflaged, others gleaming silver. I had never seen a bomber so close and was astonished not at their largeness but that they did not seem so very big, till I saw a man walking about on a wing, sweeping it with a broom.

We crawled into another tiny halt and some people got in, country people. I rejoiced in their slow East Anglian sing-song and their conversation from the sort of life I know. I had seen men working in the fields, hoeing among sugarbeet and potatoes, boys harrowing and rolling and drilling compass. I had smiled and said to myself 'That's *my* job. Yes, mate, I know how glad you are of the excuse to straighten up a minute and watch the train go by!' But it was not till I listened to the talk of these people in the carriage with me, that it came fully home to me how much my whole life now is bound up with the country pattern.

I looked down on cottage gardens, one little row in particular. There were maybe half a dozen of them all joined together, built not of Cambridgeshire lath and plaster but of Suffolk pebble. The front gardens were all alike, little mazes hedged with box, gay with flowers between. The back patches were neatly cultivated to the last square inch, peas carefully sticked, carrots feathery green, potatoes dark almost to blueness. Once again I thought angrily of town visitors who go gaily down my garden path to get some vegetables for a meal and come back, having gathered the wrong lot, exclaiming, 'How nice to get all your vegetables for nothing!' For nothing? We don't pay a penny for our seeds or our manure or the wear and tear on our tools, and of course we never put in hours out there, after a full day's work. If we took count of everything, I very greatly doubt if our vegetables come out anywhere near as cheap as the ones you buy from the greengrocer. We do get our stuff fresh of course . . . but not 'for nothing.'

As the train dawdled along with the signal against it, a hare got up not five yards from the line, loped slowly across the field, nibbling here and there, tame as a dog. A huge cock pheasant in all the pride of his spring plumage stalked majestically along the embankment. A gorse bush flamed golden so close to the train I could almost touch it as I leaned at the window, could smell the nutty scent. When did I last smell gorse? On Tunbridge Wells Common in 1937, or was it in Ireland a little later? I'd love to have a bush in the garden but it would never flourish in our cold heavy clay.

One last memory of that busman's holiday. After the ordeal of my homeward journey, I hitch-hiked into a neighbouring market town and had to wait two and a half hours. Every shop was shuttered. I was starving and parched. No restaurant at the station, but in the station yard a hut, a WVS forces canteen. I may be a country yokel but for the duration I wear the King's uniform and had the right of entry. I had a roll and butter, a meat sandwich, a big slab of chocolate cake and a cup of hot sweet tea. The cost? Fourpence ha'penny. As I handed back my cup and plate I said 'Thank you!' and I never meant it more.

# BITS AND PIECES

I SAT DOWN THE OTHER NIGHT intending to be profound, but whether it was a day out in the cold, and a too-generous tea, and the warmth of the fire, I don't know, but I found myself sitting with my feet up along the settee, my mind running on little things, on bits and pieces.

I was looking at the neck of wheat hung up beside the fireplace and gleaming silvery-gold, wondering how many people even know what these necks look like, let alone anything about them. I remember I had been reading a book about old country crafts and there was a sketch of a neck in it and of some little straw plaits such as everyone used to make to wear throughout harvest. Next day I asked Stone if he knew anyone who could make them: could his wife? He glared at me. 'That she don't,' he said, 'but I can.' He proceeded to pull some ears of nearly ripe corn and his rough fingers flashed up a couple of stalks quicker than I could follow them. In five minutes he had tossed as many different patterns into my lap. Then he sat back while I muddled about. I was all thumbs and could produce nothing recognisable by his samples. Patiently he started again while I glued my eyes to his deft fingers. Oddly enough, it was the simplest one of all, with only two straws, that defeated me longest, but next morning I did manage to take him one fair sample of each of his designs. Grudging as always, he granted that I had found the knack. It was a couple of weeks or more before I persuaded him to embark on a real neck. He had time for only about four inches, while we smoked after dockey. Knowing my Stone, I think he was not keen for me to know too much, but I took the thing home and worried over it in odd moments till I could produce something like it.

How to describe a neck if you have never seen one? Difficult. The final result is a spiral effect, fat in the middle, tapering at either end. At one end projects a bunch of a dozen or so chosen ears, while the other end curves back in a long sort of handle. You can make them any length – about two feet is usual – and the diameter at the centre is about two inches. The spiral is built up patiently round a central core of stalks. You work with cut corn just before it is ripe, yet not too full of sap, and I never can make up my mind when they look loveliest, when they are fresh made, green and silvery, or when they have dried out and are of palest gold. They combine a lovely austerity of line with the very spirit of the growing grain. Their use? None now, so far as I can find out (though Stone did say, darkly, 'Reckon they was to keep us out o' mischief, gal, time we was courting!') but they have a history mixed up with the most ancient harvest rites. Sir James Frazer in his classical *Golden Bough* mentions them and their like in various parts of the world; they were known in ancient Egypt, as well as on the Continent. In our part of the world they are regarded solely as ornaments and may be seen hanging in cottages and farms, or forming part of the Harvest Thanksgiving decorations in the churches.

I have made several since that first experimental one that still hangs by the mantelpiece. One adorned the London room of an exiled friend; another hung over the bar in a Devon inn; another by my brother's picture over the family mantelpiece. Very lovely things, these necks, and I am proud of my small part in perpetuating an old custom.

The little buttonhole braids are attractive too, though less spectacular. Each year, as the first corn is cut, I select two straws and twist up a buttonhole for myself in that elusively simple pattern and thread it through my buttonhole, tying the ends in a knot. Then one evening, maybe two months later, I walk in and toss the battered little braid down on the table and the family says 'Oh good!' knowing what it means: that I'm 'done harvest' and finished with late nights.

I've learned, too, to make primitive little bird traps with three bits of wood and a small bit of board and a brick – not that I ever use it, but

I know how. And that the best way to remove a tight-fitting wellington without soiling your hands with mud and muck is to use a short length of wood with a V-shaped cut at one end and a tiny batten underneath. You stand with one foot on the board, insert the heel of the other boot in the notch and tug. I've made several of these useful little gadgets for urban friends turned rural, and only the other day one wrote to me, 'If I haven't written, at least I have thought of you gratefully every day when I use the boot remover!'

I made a highly prized set of wooden buttons not long ago out of a broken oak hammer handle. Just sawed it into quarter-inch slices and drilled two little holes, and rubbed the slices down. Now I'm going to try and learn basket-making from one of our Italians. He has learned in camp, and has made dozens of all shapes and sizes, using the willow that grows along the brook. After that I want to find someone to show me how to make whistles out of elder. I can hollow them out and cut the notch, but I seem to go wrong somewhere with the stop.

Bits and pieces. Nothing much to any of them, yet they all go to make up life as I live it now in the country. All interesting, all needing enough element of skill and judgment to hold one's attention; all simple with the simplicity which is the basis of the most cultured taste so laboriously cultivated by those who have forgotten or who never knew what simplicity is. Am I being profound after all? Blame it all on the neck of wheat, spiralling satiny-gold in the firelight beside the fireplace.

*They stand in sturdy rows, no longer corpses,*
*but soldiers ready for battle.*

# SALUTE FOR STONE

IT WAS A SUNDAY MORNING in July and after I had had breakfast and fed the rabbits, I opened my case for a cigarette and found I was out, so I went of down to The Plough to get some. On the way I met a friend who had been ill and stopped to speak to her. She was better, and liked the new doctor. 'Yes, Stone said he was good,' I remarked.

'That was sudden about Stone, wasn't it?' she said. 'What?' I asked.

'Why, he's dead,' she said. 'He was took bad early this morning and died before his wife could get any one.'

I didn't go on down to The Plough; instead I went back home. It was a lovely morning, with high wisps of fleecy cloud and deep blue in between. Beyond my hedge rose a half-finished haystack, beside it a cart loaded ready for first thing Monday morning. Further on the corn stood, already hanging its heavy head. Soon someone would have to take a scythe and go into the field and cut round the edge to make way for the binder. How often have I watched Stone as he made the rub whistle along the blade of his scythe, testing it every now and then with his horny thumb till, satisfied, he would tuck the rub into the strap at his belt, spit on his hands, say 'Well, gal, here's luck to the harvest!' and lean forward to cut the first swathe. In a couple of minutes it would be my turn to start along behind him, gathering the cut corn into my arms and tying it in sheaves with the twist and knot he had shown me. Tiring work for both of us, so that every now and then Stone would straighten up, maybe for a pull at the blue enamel can of cold tea, maybe only for a couple of words, his cap tilted back on his damp forehead. Many a covey of young partridges he has pointed out to me in such pauses, many a field mouse's nest swung neatly between the cornstalks. Once round the field, once the binder had come clattering in, Stone and I would move on to cut round another field, not returning till each field lay flat, and when it was our job to set the fallen sheaves in shocks for drying out and carting.

Stone could never leave you alone if he was teaching you anything.

He would bully and nag till you were near screaming. Many people who knew him have asked me how I could stick working with him; sometimes I have wondered myself! But at the back of it all, my sense of justice told me he was right. He did know his job, and I didn't, and more than half his nagging was because he could not bear to see work ill done. His standard has become my criterion and till I die I shall find myself thinking of his caustic comment if ever I see farm work scamped or done amiss. Moreover, he had a nice sense of just how far he could go with his bullying and when he had driven you almost to snapping point, he would suddenly relent, toss out some grudging word of encouragement, and be as charming as only he knew how. He had the hard ruthlessness of those who work with and against nature all their lives. Many people would call it callousness, but I have never known a man essentially kinder where kindness could be of any avail. I've helped him nurse sick animals and for all his superficial roughness, he knew the right thing to do and did it. None of them died if he could save them, and none suffered if he could help it. He was the same about human beings. 'Heartless old devil,' I've heard him called, but it was not heartlessness, only a refreshing realism, and I personally have often rejoiced in his carping misanthropies.

All sorts of little memories came thronging back as I wandered rather miserably about my garden after I'd heard of his so sudden death. It seemed wholly incredible that I should hear no more of his stories, meet his sturdy little form down the lane no more, that that tough little bundle of vitality was still for ever. In the evening I felt impelled to do what I had not had the heart to do since I left the farm – I went back there, and wandered all round the fields. I went by way of the horse's meadow and along under the hedge by the path that Stone had made, that he alone used, and that would now soon cease to be a path again. I went down the cart road towards Wester Hill. The hay was cut there and lying raked into big heaps. It had got wet and would all have to be spread about and turned again before carting. A cart stood at the corner, the girth swinging from the shaft and dabbling on the ground. I picked it up and draped it over the shaft instinctively, without remembering who had taught me to do that. Similarly I stood up a pitchfork, tines in the ground. 'Never leave a fork lying down, gal. You might run your foot agin it, or a cart might go over the stele.' The barley on Eight Acres looked nice, the beans on Long Wrangles not so good; it was a thin crop, with too many thistles among it. After so fine a morning, the weather had turned sulky and a fine drizzle was falling as I made for home up the side of Middle Field and across Six Acres apple orchard, past the well we had made some three years earlier, and the pig troughs and Stone's pet arrangement of bits of tin to run water from the pump. Every inch of the way was full of that cantankerous, shrewd, lovable little devil of a man.

It was fitting that Stone who had taught me so much of realism should be the first person I should see after their death. Frankly, I did not want to see him and left the taking of my wreath till the last minute but when his son suggested my going upstairs, I did not like to say no. The first thing I noticed was his precious watch, tucked into an old inturned sock tied at the head of the bed. How many times that venerable turnip had been dragged from his waistcoat pocket to confound my optimism that it was time for dinner! As his son took the handkerchief from his father's face, two things struck me: first, how strange it was to see Stone without his cap, and secondly how he would have chuckled at 'all them lacey fallals' surrounding him in death.

At the funeral we sang his favourite hymn, 'Abide with me', and the lessons were full of his favourite sayings. You'd never call Stone a church-goer but I know few men more ready with apt scriptural quotation – even if sometimes they were not voiced as piously as might have been. Yet, though he himself might sometimes gravely question established tenets, woe betide anybody else who dared real scepticism. 'Ye're a bold man, mate,' I can hear him say to someone who expressed doubts about the benevolence of the scheme of things entire.

And so we said our farewells to Stone, under the shadow of the old church tower, the Master standing stiff as a ramrod, and the Italians close behind him, David in his best suit, young Roland a child no longer. But come to think of it, we never did say 'Goodbye' as we went our ways at the end of the day. It was always 'Cheerho, Stone!' to which he would answer 'S'long, gall!' Let it stand at that.

*Big barn: a lovely great church of a place.*

# 'ALL IS SAFELY GATHERED IN'

THE STACKYARD OPPOSITE the cottage filled up again and the threshing tackle was drawn in among the stacks, the engine chimney breathing a gentle wisp of blue-grey smoke. The leaves turned from green to gold and lemon before they floated quietly to the ground, and the fields of bare stubble lay silvery under the kindly autumn sun. The bells rang out from the five or six little churches within hearing and the village made its way by road and lane to our own church among the lime trees for the Harvest Festival.

This was my fifth Harvest Festival. I am no church-goer and in any event I was not brought up to Church of England rites, but even before I became a farm worker I had always felt the Harvest Thanksgiving service was one of the loveliest symbols in the liturgy, for harvest rites go back into the bone and fabric of mankind, long before Christianity, long before history even. So the little churches fill up and nothing will keep the people away, not even the 'awkwardest' sort of rector.

The decorations set the keynote of the whole spirit of the service. Those Cox's along the edge of the window are some of Ernie's best; their russet glory has about it nothing showy, it is just sheer worth. The fat marrows leaning at the foot of the lectern are one from George's garden, the other from Harry's rood. Harry and George may be severed by a long-standing family feud, but their marrows lean amicably against the gleaming brass beneath the widespread wings of the eagle on which rests the great Book, the purple and white embroidered silk markers curving richly from the open pages. Two sheaves are propped up against the font, and it is fitting that the sheaves were taken as they came, that the weeds were still there, tied in with the corn, symbol of our year-long fight and our ultimate triumph. That sheaf on the left came from Low Close – nowhere else does the coltsfoot riot as it does in that small corner. As I brushed past the font to slip into the pew at the back, I touched the font cover of carved oak. That was carved by the young men of the village at night school when night school meant evening classes conducted on his own initiative by the then rector in the little thatched school after work was done. They let everyone have a hand at it to get it finished for just such a Harvest Festival nearly fifty years ago and today the carved ears of corn and the poppies and the berries shine black with the touch of many hands.

The church filled up quickly. The women in their Sunday best led the children by the hand and the men filed in quietly behind them, smoothing back an errant lock of hair – so strange to see these men for once without their caps! At last the five-minute bell stopped ringing, and there was a rattle of curtain rings as the vestry curtains were drawn back and the organ changed from its rather aimless meanderings to purposeful melody as the congregation rose to its feet and voices rang out in that well-beloved hymn of triumph and praise, 'Come, ye thankful people, come!'

I doubt if most people realise how much of the Bible simile and parable is agricultural. 'A sower went forth to sow the seed' – a lovely phrase in any circumstances, but how much more real when you have yourself been one of a line of half a dozen tramping across a great, rough ploughed field, arms flung wide at every step, the grain spilling in a golden arc from your finger tips. 'The crackling of thorns under a pot' is a commonplace of daily speech but it means much more when you yourself have lit the fire, and it is *your* pot that stands precariously above the blaze so that the tea may be hot for dockey. 'With what wisdom shall he be furnished that holdeth the plough?' and looking across the aisle you see hands that held the plough before you were born, now folded decently on broadcloth knees.

I'm afraid my mind wandered rather, yet every moment it was switched back by the lessons in their order, by the prayers, the psalms, the hymns. Roland stood close behind me, a great tall fellow now, his voice fully broken, and when I first knew him he was our harvest boy, a gawky youngster with knees and seat eternally out of his trousers, his jacket sleeves always too short for his growing arms. Old Bill stood in front of me, his hair thinner than ever on top, his voice quavering but hearty, and beside him his little bird-like wife. In the next pew, on the other side, was Annie, Stone's widow.

That's where the heart-ache came into things. This was my first Harvest Festival without Stone. Even after so long, it still seems incredible that I shall never see him again, never hear his gruff voice putting me aggressively to rights, his deep chuckle as he tells some story of his ribald youth.

Now we are standing for the last hymn. Harvest Festival is not only the end of our year, it is the beginning of the next, and we give due recognition to the continuity as we sing the greatest favourite of them all, 'We plough the fields and scatter.'

And so out into the little churchyard where the sun has set and the harvest moon hangs like a great orange above Church Field. Stone's grave is at my feet, a handful of scarlet dahlias at the head. He did not help us reap this last harvest, but his memorial is in the church. He helped us drill the corn that grew into those sheaves against the font and his hand was one of those that shaped the tracery on the great oak cover. He is part of the eternal fabric of this life of ours.

*Oliver Rackham Library*
THE ASH TREE
ANCIENT WOODS OF THE HELFORD RIVER
ANCIENT WOODS OF SOUTH-EAST WALES

*Richard Mabey Library*
NATURE CURE
THE UNOFFICIAL COUNTRYSIDE
BEECHCOMBINGS
GILBERT WHITE: A BIOGRAPHY

*Nature Classics*
THROUGH THE WOODS *H. E. Bates*
WANDERERS IN THE NEW FOREST *Juliette de Baïracli Levy*
MEN AND THE FIELDS *Adrian Bell*
THE ALLOTMENT *David Crouch & Colin Ward*
ISLAND YEARS, ISLAND FARM *Frank Fraser Darling*
AN ENGLISH FARMHOUSE *Geoffrey Grigson*
THE MAKING OF THE ENGLISH LANDSCAPE *W. G. Hoskins*
A SHEPHERD'S LIFE *W. H. Hudson*
WILD LIFE IN A SOUTHERN COUNTY *Richard Jefferies*
FOUR HEDGES *Clare Leighton*
DREAM ISLAND *R. M. Lockley*
RING OF BRIGHT WATER *Gavin Maxwell*
COPSFORD *Walter Murray*
THE FAT OF THE LAND *John Seymour*
IN PURSUIT OF SPRING *Edward Thomas*
THE NATURAL HISTORY OF SELBORNE *Gilbert White*

*Field Notes & Monographs*
AUROCHS AND AUKS *John Burnside*
ORISON FOR A CURLEW *Horatio Clare*
SOMETHING OF HIS ART: WALKING WITH J. S. BACH *Horatio Clare*
BROTHER.DO.YOU.LOVE.ME *Manni and Reuben Coe*
HERBACEOUS *Paul Evans*
THE SCREAMING SKY *Charles Foster*
THE TREE *John Fowles*
TIME AND PLACE *Alexandra Harris*
EMPERORS, ADMIRALS AND CHIMNEY SWEEPERS *Peter Marren*
DIARY OF A YOUNG NATURALIST *Dara McAnulty*
LOVE, MADNESS, FISHING *Dexter Petley*
THE LONG FIELD *Pamela Petro*
SHALIMAR *Davina Quinlivan*
ELOWEN *William Henry Searle*
SNOW *Marcus Sedgwick*
WATER AND SKY, RIDGE AND FURROW *Neil Sentance*
BLACK APPLES OF GOWER *Iain Sinclair*
ON SILBURY HILL *Adam Thorpe*
GHOST TOWN: A LIVERPOOL SHADOWPLAY *Jeff Young*

*Anthology & Biography*
ARBOREAL: WOODLAND WORDS *Adrian Cooper*
MY HOUSE OF SKY: THE LIFE OF J. A. BAKER *Hetty Saunders*
NO MATTER HOW MANY SKIES HAVE FALLEN *Ken Worpole*

# Little Toller Books
w. littletoller.co.uk  e. books@littletoller.co.uk